What Was Said to Me

Also by Ruby Peter

The Cowichan Dictionary of the Hul'qumi'num
Dialect of the Coast Salish People

Thomas E. Hukari and Ruby Peter
Cowichan Tribes, 1995

What Was Said to Me

The Life of Sti'tum'atul'wut, a Cowichan Woman

Ruby Peter

IN COLLABORATION WITH HELENE DEMERS

ROYAL **BC** MUSEUM

VICTORIA, CANADA

What Was Said to Me
The Life of Sti'tum'atul'wut, a Cowichan Woman

Published by the Royal BC Museum, 675 Belleville Street, Victoria, British Columbia, V8W 9W2, Canada.

The Royal BC Museum is located on the traditional territories of the Lekwungen (Songhees and Xwsepsum Nations). We extend our appreciation for the opportunity to live and learn on this territory.

Cover and interior design and typesetting by Lara Minja/Lime Design Inc.
Editing by Helene Demers with Ruby Peter
Index by Catherine Plear

Dust jacket images

Back: Quamichan Indian Village, 1914–18. *J.W. Dickenson, Cowichan Valley Museum & Archives, 1914–1918.*

Front: Photos Unlimited, 2019.

Front flap: Ruby and Helene Demers at 2019 University of Victoria convocation, where Ruby received an honorary Doctor of Laws. *Lynsey Johnny, 2019.*

LIBRARY AND ARCHIVES CANADA CATALOGUING IN PUBLICATION

Title: What was said to me : the life of Sti'tum'atul'wut, a Cowichan Woman / Ruby Peter ; in collaboration with Helene Demers.
Names: Peter, Ruby Sti'tum'atul'wut, 1932-2021, author. | Demers, Helene, 1955- editor. | Royal British Columbia Museum, issuing body.
Description: Includes index.
Identifiers: Canadiana (print) 20210124113 | Canadiana (ebook) 20210125187 | ISBN 9780772679383 (softcover) | ISBN 9780772679406 (EPUB) | ISBN 9780772679390 (Kindle) | ISBN 9780772679413 (PDF)
Subjects: LCSH: Peter, Ruby Sti'tum'atul'wut, 1932-2021. | LCSH: Indigenous women—British Columbia—Biography. | LCSH: Language teachers—British Columbia—Biography. | CSH: Indigenous Elders—British Columbia—Biography. | LCGFT: Autobiographies.
Classification: LCC E99.C875 P48 2021 | DDC 971.1004/97940092—dc23

10 9 8 7 6 5 4 3 2

Printed and bound in Canada by Friesens.

STI'TUM'ATUL'WUT ✳ RUBY PETER

Mom

December 27, 1932–January 8, 2021

Our golden matriarch passed away on the treasured grounds of her residence, surrounded by all of her children and her loving sister, Delores. She fulfilled her mother's wish to have a huge family and was blessed with five generations of children, grandchildren, great-grandchildren and great-great-grandchildren. One of her passions as a young mother was to revitalize the Hul'q'umi'num' language for her people, and this passion continued into her last days.

Ruby was truly an inspiration to her family and many others she crossed paths with in her life. She was determined to teach Hul'q'umi'num', creating books and tools for others to learn from and follow in her footsteps. It was important to her to create many paths of learning to revitalize the true meanings of the Hul'q'umi'num' language and the traditional cultural teachings of our ancestors. This book is a part of the legacy she created for others to learn from.

What was said to her as a young lady inspired her with the dedication, passion, patience and love to set goals and work to achieve them before her passing. Her life was filled with her family and defined by her determination to document and teach the Hul'q'umi'num' language. She accepted two honorary doctorate degrees from the University of Victoria and Simon Fraser University with pride in 2019 and told everyone, "It is never too late to graduate and always be learning every day." This passion for learning and teaching anyone who showed interest extended to her family, especially her great-grandchildren, whom she cherished and who inspired her to complete the goals she set at a young age. Enjoy reading this book, as our mother shared all the words from deep within her heart.

—MOLLY PETER, ON BEHALF OF LEO, ALPHONSE,
ADELE, SHEILA, BERNADETTE AND MELISSA

Dedicated to my mother, Qwulsimtunaat (Cecilia Leo Alphonse), who encouraged me through tough times and urged me to work with our Hul'q'umi'num' Language, and to the ladies, Ellen White, Violet Charlie, Delores Louie, Theresa Thorne and Molly Hwuneem, who attended the first Indigenous Linguistics Diploma Program with me at the University of Victoria in the 1970s.

—STI'TUM'ATUL'WUT

Dedicated to all Indigenous language activists who work tirelessly to protect linguistic diversity and ensure children's rights to learn their mother tongue.

—HELENE

Foreword

RUBY PETER is the foundation of her family. She has repeatedly told her children, grandchildren and great-grandchildren the importance of cultural identity, the roots where one comes from and to learn this. Educational knowledge is vital to preserve knowledge of our Coast Salish cultural and traditional teachings. But completing your education is also important in striving for your future goals.

Ruby is my mother. I am one of four daughters. My name is Stu'matulwut (Molly Peter).

Ruby has inspired many people with her words of wisdom and by sharing traditional teachings, and recently, by receiving honorary doctorate degrees from the University of Victoria and Simon Fraser University in 2019. Ruby has shared her passion of always teaching our people to have a balance in life, complete their education, get a job to provide for their family, and teach and live our traditional way of life. She always wanted to be able to share her words with her children and offspring[1] and felt that her recording this book was one of the ways they could learn in the future: directly from her, decades from now.

Ruby voiced the importance of "never ever changing our traditional teaching or taking shortcuts, as this may shorten one's life." I have heard this directly from her and her late mother, Cecilia: to live our culture, walk with pride and share with others, as this does not belong only to us. Ruby was inspired by her mother to learn to write Hul'q'umi'num' and teach others in order for this not to be lost for the Coast Salish people. I am very inspired by her dedication and energy to never give up hope and truly believe in the goals she set at a young age. She holds love, passion and dedication in her heart, not only for her immediate family, but also for

---

1 "Offspring" refers to those directly related to Sti'tum'atul'wut.

the surrounding community as far as Yakima, Washington, and to the north, Squamish, BC, where her mother's roots are from.

This book warms her heart, as she recorded it to share words of wisdom from the many Elders she listened to as they taught or groomed her to be a mother, grandmother, great-grandmother and teacher, and it will truly inspire others to learn and set their future goals. We are very fortunate to have five generations with our mother, and every day she teaches us and encourages her off-spring to learn something. I am proud she is our mother.

I continue to work daily to take care of myself, my children, my grandchildren and my great-grandchildren, as our mother does for hers. She truly is an inspiration to everyone.

Written with love for our mother, "Ruby"

STU'MATULWUT (MOLLY PETER)
June 2020

Preface

LIFE HISTORIES are a form of contemporary social history and convey important messages about identity, cosmology, acceptable social behaviour and one's place in the world. *What Was Said to Me: The Life of Sti'tum'atul'wut, a Cowichan Woman* recounts the lived experience of a respected Cowichan Elder over seven decades and will be a valuable contribution to Coast Salish ethnographic literature. Its narrative of resistance and resilience is of interest to a wide audience, including Ruby's extended family, the Cowichan Tribes community, scholars in fields such as gender and Indigenous studies, and the general public. Ruby's life story, anchored deeply in Coast Salish territory, documents a period of profound social change and holds the potential to raise awareness of multiple perspectives and experiences, contribute to local curricula and effect change in social policy, health care and education.

I first met Ruby in 1988, when I was hired by the Cowichan Tribes Cultural Education Department to develop Hul'q'umi'num' language curriculum for the primary grades. As a fluent speaker with linguistic training and an experienced curriculum developer, Ruby, who was working as a Hul'q'umi'num' language teacher at the time, graciously shared her expertise and encouraged me (with humour) as I tried to learn some of the language. A few years later, Ruby was a frequent guest speaker in my classes at Vancouver Island University (then Malaspina University College), where she taught my anthropology students basic Hul'q'umi'num' sentences and generously shared cultural teachings. I had the pleasure of working with Ruby on a few other projects, notably a Traditional Use Study. She has been described as a Hul'q'umi'num' language activist, but her activism extends to matters of community health, housing, the justice system, environmental protection and water quality. I vividly remember her bringing a jar of water taken from the Cowichan River near her house in 1998 and inviting members of the Cowichan Valley Regional District, who were attending a meeting about the effect of sewage lagoons on the Cowichan River, to drink it.

In 1997, Tom Hukari, from the Department of Linguistics at the University of Victoria, Ruby and I received a BC Heritage Trust Grant to record and publish Ruby's life story. The grant provided a stipend for Ruby and covered her travel expenses. Ruby and I recorded her life history in English between August 1997 and February 1998. Tom recorded one of the cautionary stories told to Ruby as a child in Hul'q'umi'num', and Ruby provided the transcription (see chapter 13 for the English version). Unfortunately, this Hul'q'umi'num' recording and transcription have been lost in the intervening years. They would have been an important addition to this volume.

Once the English recordings of Ruby's life story were transcribed, we worked on the manuscript for several months, reviewing it for transcription errors, clarity and accuracy. Initially, Ruby and I had planned to publish her life story in 2001, but the prospective publisher requested that the content be reordered and arranged according to topic, while our goal—in line with oral tradition—was to publish the account as told; we wanted to maintain the integrity of the narrative and reflect the performative aspect of its telling. Publishers have a tendency to attempt to shape oral life accounts into conventional autobiographic texts, but these are distinct narrative forms and should not be conflated. A published oral life history, such as this one, is not intended to be a static, complete and sequential account, but rather a documentation of the process of creating meaning while reflecting on particular events and critical junctures in one's life (with some events repeated for emphasis).

Over the next few years, illness as well as the loss of several family members in both our families led to the project being put aside. We were also both busy with our professional lives. Ruby served on many advisory committees, was actively involved in linguistic research and continued to teach Hul'q'umi'num' at the post-secondary level and in the community. In 1995 she co-edited *The Cowichan Dictionary of the Hul'qumi'num Dialect of the Coast Salish People* with

Tom, and she continued to collaborate with him on developing Hul'q'umi'num' curriculum for post-secondary programs. She has supervised many MA projects and PhD dissertations, co-authored papers, and co-presented regularly at conferences with Simon Fraser University linguist Donna Gerdts. In recognition of her contribution to Hul'q'umi'num' language revitalization and research, Ruby received honorary doctorates from the University of Victoria and Simon Fraser University in 2019. Shortly after this, I asked her permission to submit a proposal to the Royal BC Museum with the hope of getting her life story published. Our proposal was accepted, but within a few weeks of signing the contract (with Ruby as the recipient of all royalties), the Covid-19 pandemic left us homebound, and for several months we were unable to meet to work on the manuscript and gather photographs. At the end of May, however, we finally met (outside and socially distanced) to create a work plan.

Since we last looked at the transcript there had been a Hul'q'umi'num' spelling reform, and it took significant effort to incorporate these changes into the manuscript. I worked on reviewing punctuation, checking the recordings and transcripts, digitizing cassette tapes, locating archival and other photographs and gathering permission to include the photographs in the book. Ruby checked the Hul'q'umi'num' spelling, reread the transcript and made corrections, while her daughters, Molly and Adele, and sister, Delores, searched for family photographs, and Sally Hart, manager of Shhwulmuqwqun Hul'q'umi'num' Language and Culture Collective, patiently scanned original photos. Unfortunately, the BC Archives were closed during the pandemic, which meant we were unable to access some images, newspaper clippings and documents we would otherwise have liked to include.

Aside from minor corrections, deletions and additions made by Ruby, the published transcripts are true to the original recordings. While checking the transcripts against the cassette tapes over the last few months, the "close listening" to Ruby's voice instantly transported me back to my small office on the Vancouver Island University Cowichan Campus, where we spent nine sessions reviewing and recording over cups of Ruby's favourite Red Rose tea twenty-two years ago. Ruby is a skilled narrator with a phenomenal memory and always came prepared to speak on a number of topics she had selected. These deeply embedded memories also reminded me of how all stages of life-history research are intensely collaborative and dynamic in nature: it matters where, when and to whom the narratives are told. This holds true not only of the recording process, but also of the gradual reviewing and editing that has resulted in a publication that reflects Ruby's vision of her book—a legacy for her family to guide them and, in her words, "be honourable."

At the time that Ruby and I recorded her life story, we had known each other for almost a decade, and our relationship was based on friendship and a shared interest in linguistics. In transforming the transcripts of nine recordings into a manuscript divided into twenty-six chapters, I was acutely aware of the responsibility that comes with co-authoring life histories to accurately reflect the original telling and Ruby's voice as much as possible. I initially considered a structure of nine chapters, to coincide with the number of recording sessions, but some of the recordings stop in the middle of subjects that are then picked up on the next recording. Each recording covers multiple topics, ranging from memories of her parents to reflections on challenges overcome in her adult life, and so, with Ruby's approval, I divided each of the nine recordings into shorter chapters. One of the additional advantages of dividing the book into twenty-six relatively short chapters is that this format is accessible for use in the classroom, in line with both Ruby's and my own commitment to education.

Published life histories such as Ruby's are often accompanied by academic notes or commentary by the person who recorded them. While I enjoy reading these as an academic, and while they can provide valuable contextual information, as a researcher committed to honourable practice and decolonizing methodology, I believe such notes have no place in this particular book and, at best, should be published separately. They inevitably influence the reading of the narrative and reinforce a stance of outside expertise that I find particularly problematic in documenting oral narratives. There is no need for an academic to interpret or elaborate on Ruby's life story and teachings. *What Was Said to Me* stands on its own, its message powerful and eloquent.

"Ruby's book" is the result of listening—really listening—and working collaboratively and respectfully with Ruby and her family to prepare it for publication. Ruby's story and voice live in my memory, and I am frequently reminded of the teachings she shared. Whenever I doubted that we could get the manuscript and photographs ready in time during the various waves of the pandemic, I was encouraged by Ruby's belief in setting and achieving goals—something she was taught from a very young age and instilled in her children.

When an Elder sits with you and trusts you to take their life story forward, it is an honour and a gift. I raise my hands in thanks to Sti'tum'atul'wut for trusting me with her story.

HELENE DEMERS
October 2020

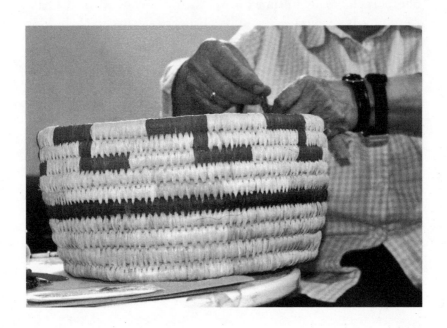

Ruby's hands on a basket she was weaving.
Shannen Joe, 2020.

Acknowledgements

THE TWO-DECADE-LONG LONG JOURNEY from recording *What Was Said to Me* to publication was like weaving a basket, gradually joining multiple strands to create a strong container to hold Ruby's story. We raise our hands to each of you who supported us in this process.

Primary funding for the recordings was provided by the BC Heritage Trust, and the book would not have been published without their financial support. Linda Love, former Malaspina University College (now Vancouver Island University) principal, generously freed support staff Marion Knost and Maureen Briglio to carry out the initial transcription. Vancouver Island University funded work study student Bethany Scott to review the transcripts and work on the first of round of punctuation—no small task in a lengthy transcript. Simon Fraser University linguist Donna Gerdts was always available for consultation and spelling, and along with PhD student Sally Hart, manager of Shhwulmuqwqun Hul'q'umi'num' Language and Culture Collective, graciously made the Language House available so we could meet in a safe environment during the Covid-19 pandemic. Sally always made us feel welcome and spent many hours scanning photographs. Her assistance was invaluable, and we owe her a debt of gratitude.

Two of Ruby's children, Hwuneem (Leo) and Sti'tum'atul'wut (Little Ruby), reviewed the publication proposal and witnessed the signing of the contract. Daughters Stum'atulwut (Molly) and Sti'tum'atye' (Adele) patiently gathered family photographs and sorted through them during meetings at the Language House. The support and encouragement provided by Stum'atulwut (Molly) and Sti'tum'atye' (Adele) are crucial strands woven into the basket. As well, Stum'atulwut reviewed the transcript with her mother, recorded her introduction and, along with Sti'tum'atye', assisted with the photo captions. In keeping with the importance of transmission of family history and knowledge from generation to generation, we asked Stum'atulwut to write the foreword.

Brian Thom, Department of Anthropology, University of Victoria, enthusiastically volunteered to make personalized maps of "Ruby's places" in recognition of the hours Ruby sat with him during his PhD research on place names and cultural landscapes, and generously sharing Hul'q'umi'num' language lessons and teachings. Four generations of family assisted in the preparation of this book: in addition to Ruby's children, her sister and close friend Swustanulwut (Delores) searched for photographs and helped identify people, and Adele's daughter, Quqtipiyè (Shannen Joe), a skilled photographer, contributed several photographs. Little Ruby's daughter, Taxwulwut (Lynsey Johnny), took the author's photo. Little Ruby's young granddaughter Kyla-lee Sxelu Hwuneem took the photo of her great-grandmother and grandmother telling the Little Wren story. Wuswasulwut's (Melissa's) daughter and Ruby's granddaughter, Stiit'i'ye (Leona Peter), Elders Assistant at the Language House, conveyed messages, reviewed the dedication for the book with her grandmother and saved the day on several occasions. Helene's son, Tyler Sage, lent his editorial eye and added clarity to sections such as the preface. When it was no longer possible to work at the Language House during the second wave of Covid-19, Helene's daughter, Jessie Demers, patiently scanned the remaining photographs. Kathryn Gagnon, curator of the Cowichan Valley Museum and Archives, kindly retrieved archival photographs when the museum was closed during the pandemic. Additional archival photographs were provided by the BC Archives. Thank you to Eve Rickert, Royal BC Museum Publishing and Catherine Plear for your patience and support during the publication process.

Baskets require a strong foundation, and even though they are gone, Ruby is grateful for the knowledge of many generations given to her by her parents, Qwulsimtunaat (Cecilia Leo) and Xitsulenuhw (Basil Alphonse).

Huy ch q'u Siem

STI'TUM'ATUL'WUT AND HELENE

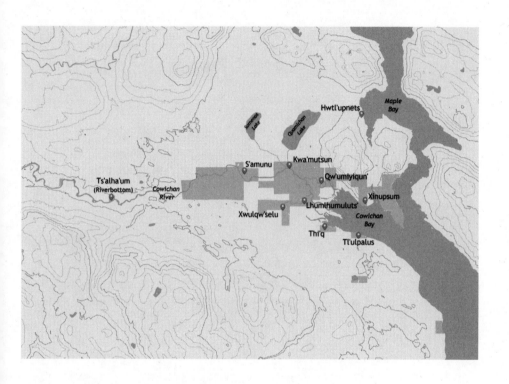

Ruby's Places. Cowichan Valley.
Brian Thom, 2020.

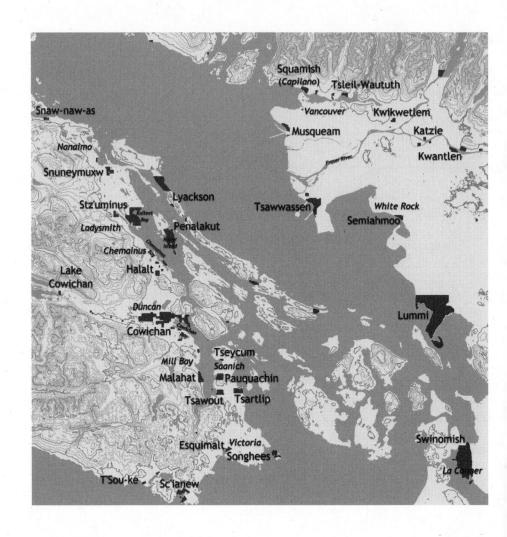

Ruby's Places. Coast Salish World (Nanoose to Sooke to Fraser River to La Conner).
Brian Thom, 2020.

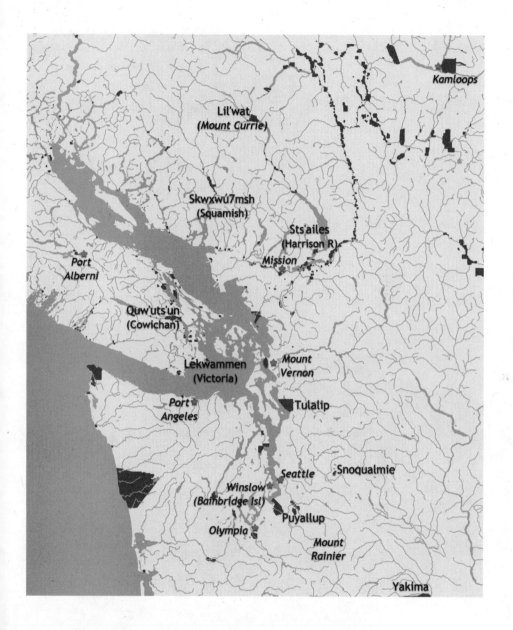

Ruby's Places. Coast Salish World (Kamloops to Yakima).
Brian Thom, 2020.

Introduction

Recorded by Molly Peter and transcribed by Helene Demers

I WOULD LIKE TO START OFF with an important message to the young people.

I have studied families, and I have heard from families that they have lost some of their culture, and writing this book might help them bring back some of the teachings that they missed out on so they can pass it on to their children, and have a better life for their children and grandchildren that are still coming up. In different families there is teachings: it's in groups, families from the beginning of time, and they know their background, and they have their own teachings of many different things—raising children or puberty time, teenagers. We have always followed the Elders' ways of teaching children, a cultural way.

There's teachings right from the beginning of time: when you first get married, when your first child comes along and how you handle that child all through their puberty time. That's another change of life. The Old People used to say, "There's many changes in life: when they are still little ones, when they are going into their teens, when they get married, when they lose parents or relations." There's teachings for every one of those. There's ways of solving problems, ways of doing things with their families. Every one of those changes, there's a cultural way. There's always someone to ask, to find out, to follow, to hear.

Children that are growing up are copy cats—how a parent acts, how they talk, how they smile, how they walk, they copy that. How they work, if they work effectively, that's how they are. Young children, teenagers, they all copy parents. How to solve things and learn about life that way. The best way to keep children from drugs and alcohol is start talking to them when they are still small, not when they are adult. When they are still small and you start talking about it and telling them the truth about what happens and how people get hurt, the damage it does to people and why it happens.

There's many, many things that we have to follow. I had a brother that read the Bible five times right through, and he said to me that everything in the Bible is the teachings of the Elders, and said, "Mom's teachings are in that Bible. Everything that you learned from Mom is in the Bible. So what you are doing is in the Bible. It's not just a made-up thing." It's a learning and following and doing, making sure that you are doing the right thing, the proper thing. And that's what life is about.

Raising children is hard. You have to watch them, listen to them, study them. How they talk, how they laugh and how you know when they are hurt, sad, when they are disturbed. That's how you study children. That's how I was with my children, if they were hurt or having problems. Even with education, going to school, I used to help them, and it really works to help them.

I went only to grade 8, and I took upgrading and I was already in my thirties. It was the young people that helped me reach grade 12. They came and assisted me and helped me, showed me what to do, because I was stuck on science. I was really stuck on science, and they came over. I was so disappointed, I was ready to quit. And they all came over—"We'll help you." I went back and I reached grade 12. There's always a way to help, to reach a goal, to help yourself, to look around. This is something the Old People always said, "Don't just sit—you watch, you listen, you hear and study what is happening with your children and what is surrounding you.

Know the people that surround you here on Earth. If you're on the reserve, families—get to know them, help them if they need help."

Life is hard, but helping young people get into a goal is the most important thing, to guide them, to encourage. You don't tell they are dumb, you don't tell that they are being stupid, you say, "Let's try it this way; let's try it another way. If you can't understand it this way, OK, let's try it another way; maybe you'll understand it this way." And that always helps when you are guiding young people: show them that they can help themselves, they can do something for themselves, that they can try harder. It's hard, but it pays off.

It makes you happy after you see what happens when somebody succeeds, when your family succeeds in what they are going for. Encouraging. Most time when young people reach their goal, they already have a family too. When they reach their goal, they have a job. They have to start guiding their own children, family to a goal that makes them somebody, makes them have a good life. A good job, that's what's important: having a job. Everyone of my family has a job, and my grandchildren and great grandchildren are following the same footsteps. Taking education. I always tell them, "Find something. If you are in one job and you are not really happy with it and you might be happier in another area, then find a training place where you can go to train to get into a better job and that's the most important."

There's always funding, federal funding, for education. Most of the time, the education that I took was federal funded. Only one was provincial funded, with a social worker to become a foster parent. The other areas I got into, they were all federal funded.

Looking for things to do for your families when they are growing up. Finding the best ways that they can get into a job. With teenagers, summer time is a hard time. My parents said, "Don't let your children just sit around and do nothing. They are going to become lazy." So they did farm work. There's labour jobs that are available for young people in the summer time. With teenagers you have to make sure that they don't get into something else that you are not happy with. Get them into sports—soccer, canoe pulling, baseball. Most of the time it was soccer for my children, and canoe races, paddling. There's really something that you have to look around for, the summer for the young people. My oldest daughter took swimming lessons, and she became a lifeguard. She was looking after young people that were down by the river swimming—that became a job for her. There's many jobs that can be had, but it is the education that's important. Most jobs, whether it's secretarial, band councillor, RCMP, bookkeeping, social work and finance. There's many kinds of jobs that can be had. Most of them take education—that's why education is important.

It is important to listen to your parents and grandparents, because of the cultural and traditional teachings that is our way of life. The cultural teachings have been important in my life. The cultural teaching I followed was right from childhood. By the time I was eight, nine years old I was already told that I can't be just playing around mixing up with many children. Both my parents were really strict on that part. The training that went with it was different and very personal, which meant that I couldn't be talking about what I was being trained for. That was the difference between a person that doesn't have any kind of cultural role to be trained for.

I was trained right from nine, ten years old, young, to understand, to know, to hear, to listen, to watch and to study people, to know what is happening. It was very strict. The young people must remember their background, their root, where they come from, who their ancestry was, their family tree. Their family tree is the most important thing to remember, to follow up and make sure you have it at all times and to give it to your children and grandchildren. That's a rule that has existed in our Native People: to know their family tree. To be able to say who you come from or the place where you came from. Know about your background. What you hold, what you have and the name, descendants of that name.

It will make me happy if you listen and hear and follow up your own traditions and our ways of life as Native People, and to know yourself and know your children, understand them, help them and give them all the support that you can give them. Find every kind of support and make sure that they have a good life and a future. And that they give a good life for the coming of the new people, new children coming up.

Huy tseep q'u. Thank you.

STI'TUM'ATUL'WUT
June 2020

Ruby's parents, Cecilia Leo and Basil Alphonse.
Courtesy of Molly Peter. Photographer unknown, date unknown.

One

MY NAME IS RUBY PETER. I am from Quamichan Reserve, Duncan, BC. My Indian name is Sti'tum'atul'wut, and they call me Sti'tum'at for short. My mother is Qwulsimtunaat, Cecilia Leo. Her childhood name was Wuswasulwut. My father was Basil Alphonse, Xitsulenuhw. His childhood name was Sal'sum'tun'. Both are from the Cowichan Tribe of Duncan.

My Indian name is originally from Squamish, way up north. My mother—my mother's grandmother was from Squamish and married into the Cowichan Tribe. Sti'tum'atul'wut was an Indian Princess, a chief's daughter, from Squamish. And this is the way it was a long time ago: that when a young lady becomes a woman, it was the parents that decided who they are going to marry. And the chief's children could not marry just anyone; they had to marry another chief's child. And Sti'tum'at was a chief's daughter. The other reason was to keep peace with other tribes. So they marry off their daughters to another tribe.

Qixuletse' was a chief in S'amun'a[1] who Sti'tum'at married. When she had children, she had three daughters. One was Agnes, who married a man in Nanaimo. The other one was Matilda. Agnes is Esther Joe's grandmother. She married a man in Nanaimo. And her daughter, whom she called Agnes, married into Cowichan. Another daughter from Qixuletse' married into Saanich,

---

1 S'amun'a also appears as Somenos.

and she left her husband, Ch'uixinukw, and came back into Cowichan and married a hwunitum', a white man. Thorne—that was Fred Thorne's father. The youngest was Ann, and that was my mother's mother. She married Hwuneem, and that was my mother's parents: Leo Hwuneem and Ann Qwulsimtunaat.

My mother was born around 1890 to Hwuneem and Ann, and lived to 1975. She often talked about her childhood with her parents. How her father had cleared up his land, how she used to follow him around as a child. She said when she was about nine years old, she used to try and help him plow the field. They used to use oxen. She said when she was about nine years old, she tried plowing. And she got behind the plow, and she was going to plow, but she was too light. When the oxen started to move, she was just thrown to the side, because her weight was—too light. Her father was telling her, but she wanted to try it, and she found out she couldn't do it so her father used to just give her the reins of the oxen, and she used to just follow along that way.

The field that they were plowing was quite swampy. She used to talk about that—some parts of it were so muddy that the oxen used to go about two feet deep when the oxen were walking, walking in the mud. Her father used blasting material to take out the tree roots. They did a lot of blasting to do their clearing. When mother and her sister became of age, they were about thirteen and fourteen, and her parents had a potlatch. And it was just announcing that the girls were coming of age. A lot of people were called to their father's Longhouse.

My aunt Emily was married at the age of fourteen, and she was given away to Alec Johnny. When a girl marries a man, they go into their reserve and they become a member of that reserve. She had married into the Xinupsum Greenpoint Reserve. My mother, Cecilia Leo, married at the age of fourteen also, and this was to a man that was from Somenos. His last name was Jimmy. So she became a Somenos Band. She lived there for ten years, and the man she was with started drinking and abusing her.

It was my grandfather's decision, when he heard that she was being abused, to bring her home. When you take someone home from a family, you have to have Elders along to speak.

Ruby's paternal grandmother, Cecilia Michel.
Courtesy of Molly Peter. Photographer unknown, date unknown.

Well-known photograph, "Cowichan Girl" by Edward Curtis,
of Ruby's maternal Aunt Emily (age thirteen).
Library of Congress. Edward Curtis, 1912.

By this time, my mother was twenty-four years old. She had been living with this man for ten years, and there were no children. She came home to her parents and stayed with them. There was another sister, a younger sister, that was living with their parents.

When Cecilia Leo, my mother, came home, she started working for different people, including helping her dad with the farm work. She started helping with the farm by plowing and disking, planting seeds. But because there was so many people watching her—she didn't like anyone watching her as she worked. She used to get up early in the morning, at daybreak, work until ten in the morning. And then she would stop and go to work—doing housework. By this time, her parents were starting to age. She stayed single for four years.

Her father had a lot of cattle and did a lot of farming. Leo Hwuneem and Ann, my grandparents, used to travel every spring to River Bottom and bring the cattle to Ts'alha'um. They had land of a hundred acres there, where they did the fishing and more farming during the spring. They even had a barn and a portable house, which is called s'iiltuw't'hw. S'iiltuw't'hw is a portable house where poles are put into the ground. Two poles close together, just enough room for a plank to slide in. So there would be like twelve poles put into the ground, and there be eighteen poles altogether, put into the ground for a portable house. A portable house—you just slide planks in between the poles, enough to bring it about six feet high, which makes it enough for a summer cottage. The planks would be about twelve feet long, and then they're just tied together as the planks are put in between these poles.

The ropes they used were made either from nettle roots or cedar. Cedar roots or cedar bark. The bark was soaked, pounded and then braided to make a rope. And that's what was used to tie up the planks to have the house built.

They stayed up in River Bottom for the rest of the summer after the planting season was done in Cowichan. And then they would go to River Bottom and do the same. Do some planting. There were about four or five families that used to go up there. And they'd have this fishing weir, which was built during the fishing season. This is also the place where they used to pick berries and sulaal (strawberries) and black caps,[2] wild blackberries, different kind of berries that used to be picked during the summer. They'd do their drying of fish and deer meat for the winter.

They used to bring up all the cattle over there, and they also had a field that was plowed and planted—a hay field. They'd come back to Cowichan after the fishing season, and then they'd do their work here in Cowichan. They used to just travel by wagon and horses. This was done every year.

The third year that my mother was home helping her father, her sister separated from her husband. Emily had three girls and a boy. When she came home, her parents were already aging. And her father told her that he did not want her moving in with them, because of the children. Grandmother had injured her back, and he felt it would be too much to have children around her. So he purchased lumber and hired someone to build a small house for his daughter across the road.

She moved into this little house with her children. Just a section for the bedroom and a kitchenette, a very small cabin. By this time, my mother had been single for three years, and she was doing all the work at home. Her father asked her to start thinking about when the parents would die. In his words, they were not well, and that his wife may not last very long because of her injury. She could not walk, she could not do anything for herself. She had to be carried. She had to be dressed. He told my mother that she should start saving up for the future and funeral expense.

This was the time when they used to go strawberry picking in the United States. So she decided that she was going to leave home for three months and put money away for the future. She left in June and went strawberry picking. And she'd come home every two weeks. She took a lot of smoked fish and potatoes, basic things that's needed, along with her so that she wouldn't spend money. She'd come home in two weeks and see her parents, make sure that they had food and whatever they needed. And she'd go back again and pick raspberries. And then after that it would be blackberries.

---

2 Black raspberries.

She said she did this for two years, saving money, blankets, making Indian blankets, swuqw'a'lh.

Then my grandfather called a meeting with his nephews, Dan Thomas and—I think that was Apil Charlie[3]—and asked them to come to his home . . . he made a will. A will for them to take care of the funeral expense. This is how the Old People used to, what they used to do a long time ago. They usually designate someone that's well off to take care of their land in exchange for other expense, such as funeral expense. Dan Thomas had asked and said that grandfather had grandchildren that his uncle should think about. And my grandfather's answer was, the children were not adults; they are still just blood. That it was the two men that he designated to look after their expenses, funeral expenses. And if any of his daughters should survive and look after the funeral expense, then the land would go to that person. And that was his wish. Even though my mother was already saving money and putting things away, he still made this kind of will.

She came back home, and it was just the following year, and her mother died. This was in 1920. It was a few years later, and then her dad died. She was very well prepared for the funeral expenses. She had three funerals close together: her father, her mother Ann and her younger sister.

My dad was already coming to see her, and helping her. This was something that the Natives always did, was helping one another. Alphonse George used to help Hwuneem quite a bit. With his son along, who was separated from his wife. It was after the funeral, and then my parents got together as husband and wife. That was in 1929.

My mother was attached to an aunt who was going blind. She was about a mile away, on Trunk Road, about a mile away from her home. She used to check her place and make sure that her aunt had the proper food. One day her aunt called her and asked her to sit down and talk to her. And she said to my mother, "You are alone

---

3 Abel Charlie, father of the late Cowichan master carver Simon Charlie and grandfather of Cowichan Elder Luschiim. The Hul'q'umi'num' language has no b sound and shifts it to a p.

Ruby at approximately four years old.
Courtesy of Molly Peter. Photographer unknown, 1930s.

now, you have no one, no more family. Your uncles are dead, your dad, your mom, your sisters—you're all alone. How come you haven't any children? You were married in S'amun'a to that man and you never had any children with him. Now you're with another man and you're still not pregnant." She told my mother that "I don't want you to be alone, I don't want you to be by yourself. I want you to have children. I'll show you what to take. If you come back tomorrow morning, I'll bring you to where we can get some medicine."

So my mother went back the next day, and she took this aunt of hers along with her to where she wanted to go. The aunt told her what to look for, and she found these four little plants. She told her that she had to take it four days after her period. The plant was pounded until it was really fine and just kind of juicy, enough to be mixed with water. And then she just drank it that way. She got pregnant the month after. She found she didn't have her period. She knew that she was expecting.

Nine months later my brother Leo was born, in April 1931. And then after that she had a baby just about every year. I was only eleven and a half months younger than my brother. I was born in 1932, Theresa was born in 1933, Alphonse was born in 1935, Delores was born in 1940, and my youngest sister was born in 1942.

Left to right: Ruby's mother; Ruby's father's sister-in-law, Josephine George, holding Ruby; unknown man; Ruby's father, holding his son Leo.
Courtesy of Molly Peter. Photographer unknown, early 1930s.

Two

IN 1940 MY YOUNGER BROTHER DIED, which was a very sad, sad occasion. My mother took it very hard. She mourned her son for quite some time.

I remember waking up and listening to her crying outside the house. I didn't understand until sometime later why it hurt her so bad. Her father had always wished for a son. And he never had any sons. And then she had a son, her oldest son, and her second son, which made her very happy. But then lost him. It was just like losing her father all over again, because he had wished for a boy so much, to take over many things that are handed down traditionally.

She mourned her son for quite some time. And I remember when she was telling me, someone had given her drinks, and she had started drinking. And then one day she said to me—and this stuck in my mind, because—she said to me that she was very unhappy. And she knew she was making her children unhappy. And to remember her words: that I should never do what she's doing, and that she was going to stop drinking. She said it makes everyone unhappy and it makes her children very unhappy. She said to me that she knew that I was very unhappy about was happening to her. She said, "Don't ever let it happen to you. Don't ever go into drinking. It just hurts more."

She said that this was going to stop very soon. And she did stop. She went back into her old self by working and working on the farm, having the Elders come to the house, and doing the things that she always did, preparing for winter.

The one that stays out in my mind, mostly as a very small child, was swinging on my dad's hand and listening to the Elders talking about their traditions, and about how the Natives became. They used to talk about all the true stories about how they came to this earth, full grown, and who was the first ones. And they always talked about the thirteen Masked Dancers and the eight people that dropped from the sky full grown. Every one of these people had names. Every one of them had stories about them. How they came about, where they landed, what they had in their hands, or if they had outfits or masks. All of these people have descendants in the Cowichan Valley. And I remember the Old People saying, they'll have to know, they'll have to remember, who they are, their identities.

With us, our family, we are from Hwuneem, and we know the background of Hwuneem. My mother used to talk about how her ancestor came to Cowichan full grown. And she kept telling us that we have to remember our background. So we have a background of having a Masked Sxwuyxwi Dancer.

We have the Rattler, which is used for different things, like marriage and pictures, showing memorial pictures. It's also used for change of life, puberty. And it is also the same for the Mask Dancers to receive their mask. The Mask Dancers can use them for memorials and weddings and funerals—adoption, if you are adopting a baby. All these things that are used; they have different songs for each occasion. These songs are handed down from our ancestors and have been passed down to the families. Certain ones from a family are picked and are given these songs and traditions, such as blessing the house with fire after a funeral or using the feathers for the new dancers.

When a widow or a widower, when they lose their mate, they have to be—we always say they have to be worked on. This means that they cannot use any sharp things, such as needles, scissors, axe, and knives, after they lose their mate. There are certain people that can work on them by singing a song and using the ochre paint on the items such as the needle, and a scissor, knife, and axe. Even the gun has to be worked on before they use it.

People have wondered why this is done. There is always a purpose for these traditions that are used. There was an example of a person that became an orphan. And this is just recently. And he came to me telling me that he could not work on anything without getting hurt. Whenever he used anything, such as hatchet, knives, he always injured himself and he couldn't understand why. He came to me because he didn't understand. So I asked him, "Did somebody work on you after you lost your parents?" And he said, "No." He said, "What is that?" So I explained to him what had to be done to him. So I told him that I do these things. So he asked me if I could do that, so I did.

And after a year he came back to me, and I asked him if he was still the same, and he said he was all right. So that showed the purpose of using the traditions on these sharp items, having it worked on before we use them.

We always say that when you lose parents, or if you become a widow, that's one of the times that—it's another new life that is beginning for the person who loses their parents or their mate. It is very important for the young people to know this: that they have to be worked on traditionally.

There are many things in life that changes a person. For the young people to help themselves by going to Elders and asking what they can do to help themselves, when they become orphan or losing a mate. It is also the same when you are growing up. What you are taught, the examples that are set upon the children, the work that they do, the work the parents do, what they see.

This was stressed on me as I was growing up. How my mother used to discipline, she was the disciplinarian. My father used to be the one to whisper at me and tell me to listen. He always said not to make my mother angry, to listen to her and to do what she said. "She will not get angry if you listen. If you don't listen, you will make her angry, and she'll spank you."

They used to travel a lot. They used to go to Indian dances. This is something that stands out in my mind, about when they used to leave. They used to go to the Longhouses, and go to the

States and different places. They used to have this old lady come in, and they used to call her Suliqiye. She was very old, with a long skirt. And they used tell us that we had to look after this old lady. "You look after your grandmother; she is just too old. Look after her so she won't get hurt. Make her tea; wash the dishes for her."

We were about six or seven years old. My brother must have been about seven. So we did as we were told. We used to look after this old lady. We used to cover the little table with a cloth—table-cloth, put the sugar, bread, teacup, bring out some jam and put it on the table for her. She'd make herself some tea, she'd have tea. We thought we were looking after her, that we were taking care of her, but she was babysitting us for two or three days. She was looking after us, but we thought we were looking after her. This was one way that our parents taught us. That was their way of teaching us, how to look after someone.

To be obedient to your parents was also stressed on us, and we were told that we had to obey our parents. Whatever we were told to do, we had to be obedient. We had to listen, and do what we're supposed to be doing while they were gone.

We respected this old lady that used to come and look after us, who we thought we were looking after. She was from Cowichan Bay, and she used to visit my parents. Her name was Suliqiye. She was an old lady with a long skirt on. She was quite heavy, but she was very gentle with us. She told us stories at night, and all she did was tell us what to do. And we did all the cleaning and the dishes and getting things ready. In the morning she would do the breakfast, but we always helped her, because we thought that she was helpless. And she wasn't really helpless; she just needed help. We got attached to this old lady, a grandmother. Whenever all the parents went somewheres, we knew that she'd be coming to visit us. If she was sick, or if she couldn't come, there was always someone that had to look after us.

This was when we were about five, six and seven years old. My oldest brother was about seven, eight. He always brought the wood in, and my dad always had wood ready to be brought in. So that was his job, was to bring the wood in. This was mostly during the winter time, when the Indian dances were going. The only other person that I remember looking after us was Xwiqw'uluq, William Thomas: he was an old man. He was called in to stay with us, and this was when my parents had to be gone overnight. This was about in 1938 or 1939.

When spring came, they always had people together, having meetings and getting ready for planting season. A lot of the people became farmers then.

One that stood out in my mind was how I used to help my mother, how I used to like to help her, because there were always a lot of people coming in and out of the house, and I used to ask to help. So she told me that I could help with the dishes. I was standing on a chair, wiping the dishes, and I must have moved around too much, and I fell off the chair. My mother was close by; she was by the fire—kitchen (wood) range when this happened. I landed on my shoulder, and she picked me up. It seemed like I was more concerned about the dish that broke, and I was hurting and crying and pointing at the dish. She helped me up, and she told me that I shouldn't do the dishes anymore. But she must have noticed that my collarbone was broken and brought it to my father's attention. My grandparents, who were always there, Sluqaliye' and Xwulqwimut—Mr. and Mrs. Alphonse George.

She called my dad and told him, and there was a discussion. And it was decided that they had to get some pitch. My dad was to go and get some pitch, the little bubbles in fir and balsam. There is little bubbles and pitch inside that, and it just kinda oozes out when you press it. So he went to get some in a cup, and he came home with that within an hour. They kept me still during that time. And then when my father returned, he had a cup of pitch. It was in a liquid form, very thick liquid. My mother had some kind of grease and put it on my skin. And then she put the pitch over the grease, and then maple leaf on it, before she put the cloth over that. And then she made a sling for my arm to keep my arm still. I kept the sling on for two, three weeks, and then I was alright after.

I wasn't brought to the doctor. They didn't really believe in doctors then. There was only one doctor in Duncan at the time, and that was Dr. Bissett.

Three

THIS WAS IN ABOUT THE EARLY FORTIES. Hard times existed among the Indians all over, because the war was on. There was a war, and that was with Germany.

I remember when people used to come around and take whatever they wanted from the people, whether they had fish or meat. We used to ask why it used to happen—things were taken away, some of our food. It was because of the war. And I guess we were lucky, because my parents had a milking cow, and they used to bury their potatoes under the house. They used to make a big pit and bury the potatoes. Put hay at the bottom of it and then dump the potatoes in there, and then more hay over it and blankets, and more hay over the blankets, to keep it for the winter. This used to help us.

A lot of people had to go without a lot of things, because they used to ration the meat, sugar, tea. And we used to have it all. I used to see my mother with a book. They called it the ration. This was a book for different kinds of food that they had to buy. They couldn't just buy sugar and buy as much as they wanted. They had to buy only a certain amount. Same with the meat. Most of the time we got our fish from the river. My dad used to go hunting, and bring home the deer meat. There was always a lot of smoked fish that were put away for the winter.

What stood out in my mind was the most scary part of that war times, was the air raid, when we used to hear the siren and they used to have the air raid. They used to have people standing outside our house, and we had to run out of the house. This was nighttime. We all had to run out. We used to ask why we had to do all that, and that was in case our house was on fire. Then we'd all go in, and if there was another siren, then someone would come around, and we'd cover the windows. My parents made sure there were nails to hang the blankets up and cover it, so there wouldn't be any light shining outside.

Alec Canute was the one that used to come around and make sure that there was no reflection of light from inside the house. He used to tell my parents that if there was any light showing, and if there was an airplane coming around, we might get bombed. It used to scare us.

This went on for quite some time. The soldiers coming around, and then the air raids. There was only one person that went into that war, and that was Clifford Gabouri. That was one of the relatives. He didn't return home after he left overseas. Ross Modeste went, and he came back, but Clifford died overseas. They talked about their prejudices when Ross came back. How they were treated as Natives when they were in the war. That it didn't exist only here at home. That they had to face people that were prejudiced against the Indians, the Natives.

After that, in 1942, they were going to let the Natives, allow them to drink alcohol. This was in the middle forties. And when they were allowed to go into the liquor—not liquor stores, beer parlours, and drink in the beer parlours. I used to hear my grandparents talking about it, that they shouldn't make it into a habit to be drinking. This bad drink, they used to call it—that it causes trouble.

There were a lot of the Natives that wanted to be able to go into the bars and drink. And there, a lot of the older people who were objecting to it, because of the trouble it will cause among the Indians. How bad it is, and how it warps their minds, and that they could never think straight. This is what I used to hear from the Old People, talking about how alcohol would be causing trouble to the Native People. That it didn't belong to the Natives. They always said that they can have a nice time without alcohol. Get together with one another without having to have something that causes trouble for them.

A lot of the Elders objected, and there were many meetings in the Band level. I always heard the Elders talking about the meetings that went on. How the older people objected to the liquor law, and how the younger people wanted to be able to go into the liquor stores. And then they talked about enfranchisement. And a lot of the people wanted to take that. And I heard my mom and dad talking about it, that if we take enfranchisement then we'd lose our status, that we'd never be able to live on our reserves. That we'd have to move off reserve. They talked about five or six people that were thinking about taking this just so they would be able to go into the liquor stores. There was about four, five people in the Cowichan area that became enfranchised. And I heard my parents and grandparents objecting to this, because they'd lose their status.

I remember when the Old People were talking about—my parents, grandparents—talking about this Indian Act Number Three, Number Four, and what would happen. I didn't really understand at all what that meant, but they mentioned that if we go on Number Three or Number Four, there was always something that they'd lose. And I didn't understand why there were numbers that the Native People had to take—which number Act that they had to choose.

There were many things that went on in the early forties. It seemed like it was all just about at the same time things were happening with the children. They talked about the children that were being taken away from the parents, and it always seemed to have something to do with the Indian agent. The Indian agent would be going with a policeman to different homes and taking the children away. The children were brought to Kuper Island, Mission, Port Alberni and Kamloops. There were different residential schools that they were being brought to. My sisters, Delores and Molly, and my cousins, Violet and Rose, were taken to Kamloops Residential School.

My parents talked about it, and they made sure that my brother went to school locally. They said that if he was in school then they'd leave him alone, but if the children were kept at home,

KUPER ISLAND INDUSTRIAL SCHOOL

Kuper Island Residential School, one of eighteen residential schools in British Columbia. Many Cowichan children attended this school, including Ruby's father and the children's father. This is one of the many reasons why Ruby wanted to revitalize the language and culture for future generations so people can hold onto their inherent rights.

BC Archives. Photographer unknown, 1913.

then the agent would go into the home and take them away and bring them to a residential school. A lot of the children were just whisked away from their homes without any notice to the parents. They just went into their homes and put the children in cars and bring them to whichever residential school they wanted to bring them to.

A lot of the children weren't able to come home during the summer. They were brought to the residential school, and they'd stay there four to five years. And some of the children did come home. I couldn't understand why some didn't come home at all, if it was the parents that didn't go for them, or if they were just not released from school. We just heard a little bit from different kids that were coming home. I found out later that the children had low-grade education because they worked on a farm instead of going to school.

My parents heard a little bit—there were whispers about abuse and things like that. Some of our relatives, cousins, that were sent over there. My dad talked about going into residential school, to Kuper Island, that he was there for three years, and he had only grade three education. A lot of the older people were in residential school and had a three, four, five, grade five education.

I used to ask my dad where he went to school and he just said, "Kuper Island." He didn't talk about what happened to him there. Every time I asked him, he just kind of avoided the questions about how it was there. He just said he didn't like it. He didn't tell me if something had happened there. My mother wasn't allowed to go to school. My grandfather didn't believe in her going to school, so she did not have any education at all.

I did notice that a lot of the Elders knew how to read. Some of them knew how to read, and some of them didn't know how to read. All the ones that went to residential school knew how to read. We asked some of the Elders where they went to school, and some of them went to Mission, some of them went to Port Alberni. There are residential schools in Kamloops.

I've heard from some of the ones that were in residential school in the 1940s, early '40s, how bad it was, the abuse that went on in the school.

Four

WHEN WE WERE AT St. Catherine's School—we started at St. Catherine's School[1] in 1938. And it was all nuns that were teaching. There were about six sisters that were teaching. They used to teach us—we always started the day with "Oh Canada!" and then prayers. Then we would go into our classroom and do our catechism, and then we would go into our schoolwork. In the afternoon we'd have home economics.

My mother didn't mind our doing home economics, learning how to sew and learning how to knit. But some of the Native Indians, one lady used to go and get mad at the sisters, because she said she was teaching her children how to knit, and that the knitting that they were doing—that they were just taking the knitting and selling it. That was what she kept saying. But it always happened that when she was there, my mother was there also, and my mother would be telling her that she didn't mind. She never had the time to teach her children how to knit. And she'd be telling the sisters she didn't mind, and this other woman was really complaining and mad at the sisters.

My mother was a very busy person. They were always doing things and going somewhere and working, but she always made time to teach us, tell us things about what we belong to—which I

---

1 St. Catherine's Indian Day School in Duncan, BC.

St. Catherine's Indian Day School. Like residential schools, Canada's Indian day schools were operated as a government and church-run initiative to assimilate Indigenous children. There were one hundred day schools in British Columbia. Ruby's sister Delores is in the third row, fifth from the right. *Courtesy of Molly Peter. Photographer unknown, mid to late 1940s.*

really didn't understand at the time. That there was some things that she didn't want us to be.

I never understood why she didn't want me playing with the children. She said that we were special, and she didn't want me to be playing ball and softball, or any other games. Even when I was small, six, seven years old, she used to tell me that I shouldn't be playing, that playing softball was just practising laziness. And I couldn't understand why it got me lazy. But later on I understood what she was saying, but at the time, I was too young to understand.

Even though she wasn't there, I didn't participate in playing. I played with the children, girls, but we were told we were not to play with boys. We played tag and things like that. But when it came to softball, I didn't participate, because of what my mother was saying to me.

I used to spend a lot of time with the smaller children, the ones that were just starting school. I was seven, eight years old then, and I'd stay with the six-year-olds and talk to them. But we had to be teaching these children to speak English, and not to speak Indian. We weren't allowed to speak Indian at all.

There were about 120 children at this day school. there were quite a few children from all of the reserves: Koksilah, Green Point, Cowichan Bay, Clem Clem, Somenos, Quamichan and Co-wichan. There was seven reserves where these children came from. And they were transported by bus. We had to catch a bus at eight in the morning and come home about four o'clock in the evening. We were always the first ones to get on the bus and the last ones to get off after school.

We always worked along with our parents at home, helping with the chores. Even though we were going to school, we still had chores to do. When I was about eight years old—and this was a sad time. There were five of us, Leo, myself, Theresa and Gordon and Delores was born in 1940.

That fall, September in 1940, we had a lot of fish, and we were cutting fish that day. And my mother used to cut fish really fast. And I would be washing the fish, washing it and cleaning it and throwing it to her, towards where she was. It would be—put it on top of fern. She always made sure that I had a lot of fern picked, and then after the fish is washed, you throw it on the fern so it wouldn't slide around and wouldn't get dirty. She had a board that was nailed together, and was in sort of a V shape, and she used to cut the fish so fast on this board, open it, and then would salt it a little bit and then hang it up for drying. This was in 1940. My dad used to do all the hanging of the fish, splaying the fish, and hanging it up. I did the washing and cleaning, scraping of the fish slime for my mother to open. My dad had a woodshed built, and we used to use that to dry our fish. Fill it up with salmon. Hang up the salmon in there to dry.

They used to use fishnet to catch the fish. This was after they stopped the weir, and it was against the law to use the weir. And they allowed our people to use a fishnet to catch fish.

We were doing about 150 fish.

And it was during this time that my younger brother was sick with pneumonia. Mother had made sure that he had stayed in bed and that he was not to come out of the house. Theresa, my younger sister, was with him. And it was about eleven o'clock; we were just about more than half way finished with our fish that we were doing. And my little brother came to the door and was calling to us. He was speaking in Indian and saying to look at him, that he was alright. My mother turned around and she told him to go back and go back to bed. And he just called to us again, saying he was alright. And she said, "Go back to bed," and he must have didn't listen.

I continued washing the fish, and then we both looked, and he was running towards us, right through the middle of a pool of water. It had been raining the day before, and there was a pool of water not too far from the garage. And he threw himself right into the water. My mother washed her hands—quickly washed her hands—and she went to pick him up, and she went inside. She told me to continue what I was doing, and then she went inside and changed his clothes and dried him and tucked him back into bed. And she came back and she said that he was still fevering. There was no one with him, just my sister, Theresa. And she was told to stay with him. She tucked him into bed, and she came back outside. And this was around eleven o'clock. And we had about, maybe another 50 fish. So she continued cutting up the fish, salting it and hanging it up. By eleven thirty, or just before twelve, we had finished doing the 150 fish. And she washed her hands, and we just cleaned up what was there—bracken fern. Dad threw away the fish guts, and we cleaned up around where we working.

She went inside the house to see our brother, and she said he was worse, so she called dad and told him. Dad cleaned himself and they all got ready. And this was before one o'clock. And they left for the hospital, or to the doctor. I don't know where they went to; I just knew they were going to a doctor. I was left in charge of the other children. And two hours later, when they got home, it was about two o'clock—and they said that my brother had died. My mother was crying, my dad was crying. And I just wouldn't believe that it had happened. I just sort of waited, thinking that it wasn't true, what they had said, that our brother had died. Mother kept crying and crying, and then I just realized that it was true. It was a very sad moment for all of us. My sister Delores was a baby, and we just didn't know what to do. They had a funeral four days later. With funerals you have to, when somebody dies, on the fourth day you had to bury the person. And this is what happened. On the fourth day, they had a funeral for my little brother.

It seemed like just after that, then, that I was left with my little sister most of the time. My mother was in mourning, crying every morning for it seemed like a long time. We'd find her at daybreak, and we'd hear her crying. Dad would take walks then. I'd follow him, but he would say to go back. And I knew he was crying.

I couldn't understand why my brother died. It was quite some time later before I found out. I just knew my parents were upset, and they constantly cried. It was later when I found out that my brother had double pneumonia. He already had pneumonia, and he came out when he was calling us and telling us he was all better. He was only three years old, but he spoke very fluently, and he was very outspoken at his age.

I know that losing a son was very hard on my parents, especially my mom. When her father had children, he had all girls. And he constantly talked to my mother about having children, and if she should have a boy to take his place. Not a boy, but boys. So my oldest brother was named after my grandfather, who was Leo. So when her first child was born, she called him Leo. And her second son, who was named after Alphonse George, my dad's father, so he was named Alphonse. He was three years old when he died of double pneumonia.

The hardest part in losing a brother was listening to my mother cry, and my dad going by himself and crying for the boy that they lost. The reason why my mother took it so hard was her dad always talked about that he wanted to have somebody to take over his name from the family. Because he had only girls, and he wanted somebody to carry on with his name and the traditions that he held.

My younger brother was a great loss to my parents. They tried to carry on their lives, but it was hard. And, I guess, someone tried cheering them up by giving them drinks. And then they went into drinking for a time. We found ourselves by ourselves. The children, my brother, myself, Theresa, Delores, were by ourselves.

And then one day, I complained to our mother, and said to her that we were hurting. She sat me down—this I will never forget—because she sat me down and said to me that this was not going to carry on, this is going to stop. "I know I'm hurting my children that are still with me. I will stop. But I want you to remember this: alcohol isn't the way to cure something when you're hurting. You remember that you're getting hurt by my drinking."

And she promised me that she was going to stop. She and my dad did eventually stop and carried on with their lives.

Five

THEY WERE FARMERS. So that farming became something that we had to be doing all the time. Working with horses and plows. And we were being taught how to feed the animals and things like that. It was my mother that always sat us down and talked to us. My dad was always busy farming, working in the field. He never came in until late in the evening, just for supper. When he came home—he was working full time, going out to work and coming home, doing plowing and then coming home late. After supper he'd be gone again, doing farming. So, it was always my mother that sat us down and talked to the children.

The teachings always seemed to come when we were busy in the kitchen with my sisters. It was mostly me, because I was the oldest daughter. And she always talked to me and told me that what I see, to remember, the work that goes on around me, and that someday I was going to get married. But to remember that "it's only that if you work. And it's going to be the teachings that you'll have to remember, the things that I teach you." These were always what she said, "What you learn from your parents is what you are going to have to pass down to the next generation."

I always got upset when she said that I was going to get married. I always thought that I'd never get married. And she always told me, "You're thinking you're not going to get married, but you are going to get married." It always made me kind of angry, because I thought I didn't want to get married. But she always kept on talking about the teachings of how you teach children. And I thought, "Why is she telling me these things when I'm only nine, ten years old?" She kept talking about that I have to learn the traditions.

And this was something that she always said, what she was going to hand down to her children: that I have to start learning at an early age, and that I can't talk about it to anyone. That I have to keep it to myself and not tell other children or talk about it. She used to say, "Only certain people hold the Sxwuyxwi Mask. And I'll be telling you all the stories about what you hold, where it came from, and that someday you are going to give it to your children."

She always had something to teach me when we were working around the house. She was very strict, and a perfectionist. Things had to be done a certain way, as quickly as possible. You had to do it fast, and you cannot make a mistake. That it had to be done properly. And she always said that, "If you do something proper, then that will be you. You'll be doing the same thing. Whatever you do, you'll do it properly. If you do something now and not finish it, you'll be like that for the rest of your life. You will not complete anything; you will just do things halfways and let it go. So what you do now is for your own good, that you will be doing for the rest of your life."

I always felt that it seemed like every day was like a lecture, but she always told us stories about what can happen to us. Like when we used to go school.

We used to walk to school, about three miles away. We used to come home for lunch, run home, and then run back to school, because we didn't have any lunch money. There wasn't quite enough money to go around all the time. She was always constantly saving money for something: a tractor, equipment, a car. There was always something where the money had to go to, to keep our lives going. And she always said that that was setting an example, that things had to be done. Especially that she had cattle. She had about one hundred heads at one time.

She was always a foster mother. She raised her nieces, and they eventually left her and went to the other grandparents. She had other nieces that stayed with her. And when she got with my dad,

dad's younger brother stayed with my parents. They had a lot of work going with the Old People. There was always involvement with Elders. The farm wasn't only in our area, it was with other people. People that were close by, and four or five miles away. It was just horse and plow and disk when I first realized what my dad was doing, that he was farming. Horse, wagon, disk, plow—all had to be put on a wagon, and they brought it to the neighbours to help them work, because they were helping one another. They were just like a company; when they did something, the people came to help them. And when they needed plowing, my dad went to plow for them, and disk-planted their potatoes or vegetables. They, in turn, helped by bringing in the hay. So there was always work, all year round. This was on the side, after my dad came home from logging.

I think my dad worked all the time. He was falling—logging trees. In the earlier part of his life he was over in Winslow, Washington. He used to leave, and he never came home for a month, and he'd come home to visit. We always waited for him. And the Old People didn't like this, my dad being away from the family. There was this old man, William Paul, he was a Shne'um or shaman. And he had put his son in the Longhouse, but his son went after the dancers with a gun. That was one time. And another time, he had a knife. And the third time, I can't remember what it was that he used, I think it was a gun again. And then he said—I overheard them talking in the Longhouse, that they were going to let this man go, because he used a knife and a gun, and threatened the dancers, so they let him go. This was in December.

And then around January, this uncle talked to my grandmother and grandfather. He told them that he wanted my dad to take his son's place and my mother had asked my grandparents not to do that. But my grandparents had already agreed with this old man to take his son's place. Because this old man was very, very close to my dad. So they phoned my dad and asked him to come home. And when he came home, we already knew, because I had overheard the Elders talking.

My sister, Theresa, was about four or five years old, and I was telling her what was going to happen. So I was telling her, "You tell Dad to get away from the dancers. They are going to put him

34

in the Longhouse." So Theresa went over to my dad, and she started crying—she was a good actor—she started crying, she said she needed to go to the bathroom, because it was outdoors then. My dad picked her up and took her out and I was walking behind, and I kept telling Theresa, "Tell Dad." I was speaking Indian to her. And Dad wouldn't listen, and Theresa kept telling him, and he still didn't listen. And then just then, I looked back, and I noticed somebody with a black face behind me. And I thought, "Oh, they're smart. There's somebody here; I can't talk." So I didn't say anything, and I hoped that Theresa would talk to my dad. But she started crying again. She tried talking, and she was just getting scared, and she couldn't really tell him.

We went back inside, and then my dad was initiated in the Longhouse. Because of the term that is used among our people, when they initiate someone, they say that they are going to "kill" that person. We thought that it was really saying that they were going to kill someone, but it wasn't, that was the initiation part of the Longhouse. The reason for the word they use is because of the new life that is given to them when they are initiated into the Longhouse. When we used to ask about the Longhouse, they used to tell us, "You cannot talk about the Longhouse. If you want to know about answers about being a dancer, you'll have to become one." And it is still the same to this day. People that question about the Longhouse are always just told that they have to join into being initiated to be able to understand what happens in the Longhouse.

I remember when they initiated my dad. My brother, Leo, was eleven, but he was really upset about what was happening to our father and what they were doing. He did not understand because of that phrase that people often use about that they are going to kill him and that is just a phrase used in the Native language tongue to say that they are giving him another life, another beginning of life because at the beginning of that four days, four nights is very important.

The four days that the person is in there they do not talk to anyone; they talk only to the dancers that are doing the initiating. Things that are done become very personal to our Native People. There are four days that they don't eat very much, they go only to the bathroom, and that is about all. They are kept sequestered from everyone, and no one talks to them. They do have certain Elders come forward to talk to them in our Native tongue, to let them know why they are there. It is usually an Elder that does that, and it is really to calm the person down who is being initiated so they would not run away.

When they do get initiated, they have to be in the Longhouse for at least three months. I think about two months is about the shortest, not one month, two months would be about the shortest to be in there, and they travel to all dances that are on the Island and across to Vancouver, Chehalis, Harrison, and then it goes into Lummi, La Conner, Tulalip and back to the Island. They have gatherings such as honouring families or memorials, and people are called to these places. They are invited to different places for memorials.

The memorial that we have, usually the person has to be deceased for about four years before they are honoured with a memorial and their pictures are shown to the people. Before they started using pictures, they used to make a little doll from the goat's wool to represent a family member who is deceased, who has been deceased for four years and a doll would be made from goat's wool and make it look like a little doll. The last doll that was done was by Adam Jimmy's mother, and she had a memorial of three people who were adults. There is a picture of that memorial that was at the Provincial Archives. The dolls that were made were made to look like adults by having a hat and a doll big enough for the hat to be put on them. That was put on a canoe and the canoe was set down and blankets were put in there and then the dolls were set down into the canoe a certain way so they'll face the people. This is brought around to the people, and they are told who this doll represents. She was the last one to have these goat's wool dolls as a memorial. After that, they have been using pictures of people that have passed away and they use their pictures to show. Before, if you were going to have a memorial of someone, especially people that really get hurt about looking at somebody's picture, like a son, a daughter, a mother, or any family member.

I remember my grandmother when we were visiting her and then her daughter had passed away, my dad's sister, and what happened was there was a picture that was always covered. I asked my dad why was the picture always covered, and that was a picture of my aunt who passed away, and my grandmother would always cry if she looked at the picture so she covered it. After the fourth year, the picture was shown and brought out to the people. A memorial was given of her, and then the cover from the picture was taken off and it was put out in the open. My dad explained to me that my grandmother had finally let my aunt go to her resting place and to continue her journey in the next life by letting her go and then looking at the picture with love and not crying about her. The explanation, they said, was that if you cry for a person all the time, you are keeping them in this world and not letting them go to the next world, you are holding them back and not letting them rest. This is mostly the purpose of showing the picture to people and having a memorial, to release your loved one on their journey to the next world—to let them go.

Six

THE THI'THA has a lot of responsibility of people that become orphans. When a person young or old becomes an orphan, a widow or widower, they have to go through a lot. For sharp things, which has to be done in the morning, a song goes with it—a prayer song—and it's for the needle, knife, scissors, axe, and even the gun have to be worked on. The purpose of this, having orphans, widows or widowers being worked on, is so they won't injure themselves if they use sharp things such as needles or knives or anything that is sharp. The prayer song that goes with this, the ochre that is put on the needles, scissor, knife, axe, and the gun and also the paddle for people that paddle or people that cross water, so that nothing will happen to them when they travel. If they cross the water, they have to walk into the water with sq'umul (paddle) and tumulh (ochre) on their foot and on their leg. There is always a song that goes with this, a prayer song.

Each individual person that is a Thi'tha, the one that does this work, have their own songs that has been handed down to them from their great-great-grandparents, whether it is from the male or the female. When they are taught these songs, they have to know exactly what to do. They have to learn the words from their parents, learn the words, what it means and learn what to do.

Fish and seafood also have to be worked on. The purpose for the fish, because as Native People we always eat fish, and the seafood is because the fish travels in the water, it has to be worked on, and it's all the same prayer, song or "wordpower." Each individual Thi'tha is taught what to do and how they do it. With the dry fish, what is used is the eagle down, grease and ochre paint, and there is a certain way of putting it on the fish. There are different ways of working on the seafood. There is a certain kind of plant that is used that's got all the thorns on it and it is put through octopus. The octopus is boiled, and then it is the same thing that there is a song that goes with it. This thorny stick is usually put through the octopus, and then the person eats that; the same with the clams and the deer meat. If you don't want to do any of these things, you would have to go without eating these foods. If you don't get worked on, then you can go without them for a year. Like the fish or seafood, you can go without eating it for a year.

The Thi'tha has a lot of responsibility; after the funeral they also can burn the clothes of the deceased. There is always a set of clothes, the person that dies, their favourite clothes what they wear every day; so there is four sets of clothing that they wear every day from shoes to their underwear and their shirts. If it is a man, it is pants, shirt, shoes and socks, T-shirt if they use T-shirt, and a jacket, and that is what is burned. If it is a lady, it is the same thing, if they have a favourite jacket, you use a favourite jacket. There is usually four different sets of clothing that they wear if they have a favourite clothing that they use for going out, like going to a dance or going to party, then that is burned too.

The burning of food is never done right away when a person dies. The explanation that I got for that was that when a person passes away, they do not wish to have any food because they just feel lost and they don't know what happened to them. My mother used to advise people not to burn food right away, because it will be somebody else that will come to it and take it. She said that it became kind of dangerous because you may not know these others that will come for the food. Time has changed, and I have told some people what I was told. Even the cutting of hair after the funeral for the orphans. We used to cut their hair.

The Thi'tha has also the responsibility of the new dancers. A lot of things in the Longhouse that goes on there, the Thi'tha is usually the one taking part in what goes on in the Longhouse.

There aren't too many people that have the complete gift from their ancestors. A lot of our people didn't think too much of it and never accepted their gift from their parents and grandparents. Because of this, it is lost to them. There are very few young people that have accepted this gift. At one time there was three or four to each village right from Nanaimo to Victoria.

I remember one time when my mother was called to Nanaimo and the burning of food for the Longhouse and all the people that were Thi'tha from each reserve. There was about twenty-four tables of about one hundred plates on each and they, each one, would have to look after their table. The food that was prepared for the burning . . . it was just so much food that was put on the table for these people that have passed away. It was just like one great big party for them, and the people that were called were two from each reserve, from Nanaimo, from Ladysmith, from Cowichan—there was usually four or six that were from Cowichan—and there was about four from Chemainus Bay area, four from Nanaimo, four from Malahat, Westholme. It became sort of a competition to see who had the strongest prayers, wordpower; which one was going to burn properly. Who had the power of prayers to have this food be accepted from the people that were beyond, that have been gone for many years, and to feed people that have been gone for many years. These people that were Thi'tha that had this power to do things, to feed people that were beyond, in another world, call them to accept food that were in this world.

It was really something to see all these people that were Thi'tha.

My mother used to tell me that I was going to be able to do this: "You are going to know. Don't be impatient about your powers that you are going to be receiving. You will know, you will feel, you will hear and you will know what to deliver when the time comes. I am not going to be here to show you, but you are watching and learning and you hear." And I thought, "Well, I guess," waiting and thinking, wondering whether that was true or not. I was told never to question anyone, never to question my mother of things like these that I will find out for myself or any of the things that were done by the Thi'tha. She always told me that each Thi'tha has their own wordpower, how to go about things, about what they do and how they do it. They are taught and they have to learn, and they have to use it the proper way and learn from the Elders. It was a time before, after my mother died, and I took complete control of all the things that she used to do. By this time, I had learned right from my childhood to the time she died, learned everything she knew. Only because I was the oldest girl. My brother was older than me, but he did not feel that he could carry through, so he more or less left it up to me to take over all of the things that Mother did.

The training was just gradually from childhood, the teachings. It seemed like a day never passed without her telling me something about what was going to be in the future; things that we had to learn, the things that I had to teach my children, and with the carrying of this very entrusting. I thought that everyone had this kind of gift. It was much, much later that I learned that the gift that was given to me wasn't for everybody. She said it to me. She told me, "This is only for your ears; it is not for anybody else. You listen." She always said to listen. The learning part, I didn't think it was so much.

I never counted, how much she taught me, what she taught me; and then it wasn't until recently I started thinking when I started passing it on that I realized what I am passing on to my children. What they are going to be carrying for me and their great ancestors that were ahead of us. And then I thought, this is when I really thought about what the greatest gift that we are holding and are passing on to the younger generation. The gift that they are receiving is just such a beautiful blessing gift that they are going to be passing to their children. So a Thi'tha is someone that is very important to the community.

Seven

THE RATTLER is another that is held by different people. Not all Indians hold the Rattler. This was a gift from my grandfather that was passed on to my mother; and there are a lot of teachings to the Rattler. Also, how you look after it, how you look after yourself, what you use it for, whether it is for memorial, whether it's for new dancers: combing their hair, or bringing someone in who is going to receive an Indian name. The Rattler that we hold can do a lot. It can be for memorials, for Indian names, it can be for bringing Elders in for a blessing from the Masked Dancers. There isn't that many that hold the Rattler. There is a song that goes with it. Each individual person that has this has their own songs, and these people can hand it down to their children. It is up to the person that has the Rattler to pass it down to the next generation. It cannot be passed to a stepchild, but it can be passed to the family member. They can use the Rattler for many occasions. Also, when a young lady has a change of life, to bring them in, and maybe the Mask Dance will bless them after. The Shne'um is different. OK, the Rattler is the Tth'uxwten, you can call the Rattler the Tth'uxwten. That's part of your Tth'uxwten. The Rattler and the Masked Dance are part of your Tth'uxwten. The Masked Dances are inherited by families. It is only the families that belong to the Masked Dance can hand it down to another family member. It is only if you have received a Mask from your ancestor and then you can pass it down. You cannot pass down something that you have never received. You cannot just say that, "Well, it was given to me, but I never received it." If someone gave it to somebody, they would have to have witnesses to say that. If a person has witnesses that it was given to them, it would have to be three or four people to stand up and say, "Yes, we heard this Old Person saying that she was going to pass down the Mask to this person."

A person cannot just take a Mask; it only belongs to a family tree, and the family has to know the background of each Mask that they have, where it came from, where it originated from, who was it handed down to, the name that receives the Mask, the one that is receiving the Mask and the songs. Their name has to come from someone that's a descendant of the Mask. A long time ago, they never used to give a Mask to people that belong to the eight; they could not hold the Sxwuyxwi and the Hwte'tsustsus Rattler. These are a group of people. They are a separate group of people from the ones that have the regular Rattler. The Hwte'tsustsus, they have only one person singing for them if they bring a group of people or one person into the Longhouse for whatever they do. There is a group of eight people, whether it is a canoe, picture, person or naming. They can use the eight, but it is only one person out of the eight people that will sing a song. The one they call the individual Rattler, which I belong to, they have their own individual songs and when they use these people, there has to be two people or four people to bring one person in.

Each individual Rattler will have their own song. They are never identical songs; they are all different unless they are from the same family tree. Even when they are from the same family tree, same family song. Family songs can be identical and when it is given to another family member, sometimes the song changes just a little bit. It is still the same song, but it would be sung just a little bit different. When my mother gave the song to my sister, I was thinking my sister wasn't singing it properly because she sang it a little bit different, and then my mother said, "No, don't stop her. This is how she is going to be passing that song to her children." The way she sings it, it's got the basic meaning how it is sung, but the sound was a little bit different; the same sentences, but how she sang it was different from the way that my mother sang it and it disturbed

43

me, but she said, "No, let it go, that will go on with her family tree because your sister has a family, her children, and that's how she will pass it on to her children." It took me a while to understand what my mother was saying that the song that she was passing to us. She gave it to all of her four girls, and we all sing it almost identical, the same sound, the same sentence, but the ending part of it was a little bit different with the other two sisters. I have given it to my daughters, and the same thing is happening with what my mother said. It is the same sentence, but one daughter is singing it just a little bit slightly different from the other sister. Now I realize that what my mother had said about the songs, as long as the meaning is there of what the song says. The most important one is the meaning of the song and then the way it is sung by the individual person. I am also passing the song to my children in the same way that my mother had passed it down to her children. All the girls sang the song, but her oldest son, who is our only one brother, and he is the oldest one of us. He never did use the Rattler or sang the song. When mother was very ill and was sick, she had said that two of the strongest one of her siblings, children and grandchildren, that this will be passed on to them and then my brother did not teach his children. He asked me, and continually asks me to pass down the Mask and the Rattler to the children of his choice that he wants, and I have passed it to my children.

I have spent time studying my children, nephews and grand-children thinking of who I am going to pass things to. I have made all the young people in our family aware that they can inherit the Rattler, the Mask and the different things that was handed down to me. Now, it is not only my children, it is my brother's children also that I have to think about. I still have to bring them together and talk to them and tell them who it is going to; not so much as telling them who it's going to go to, but telling them that they have to be aware that only those that keep themselves in proper manner to the community, to be upstanding members of the community and to follow the ways of our Native People in helping one another. What my mother had said was to watch yourself, to keep yourself in a proper manner, to behave properly to the people and to the whole Native community, to be helpful to them for sadness or happiness. To be always showing yourself and showing that you can participate in many things in doing only good deeds; not only to your family but to the whole community. It is an important role for our members of the family to know this. To remember who they are, who they represent, and why they have to be in a behaved manner; that they cannot be causing trouble or bringing trouble to anyone. This is something that we were taught very early in our age, that with holding a lot of things we have to be very, very strict with our young people, our children, and to let them know.

This is something that I have done to my own grandchildren, talking to them, telling them who they are and what they are going to hold, what they are going to be when they grow up, and this is something that I told them was very important that they do not talk about it to the public to the other Native children. This is something that I have taught my grandchildren. They cannot say that "I hold the Mask, I hold the Rattler, I do the Cleansing of the House." We do not talk about it to anyone. We have to keep it to ourselves, and this is what I told my grandchildren. I was very surprised that they had listened so closely, that when they got home, they told their mother that they could not tell them the secret that I had told them, and that was the secret for them to not tell anyone what I had said. I find that this is very important to tell them at a young age, and that was the same thing that I was taught as a child, that you cannot be throwing it to anyone, that I belong here, that I belong to this, I belong to the Rattler, or I belong to the Mask or any of things that we hold. We have to be very closed. We don't talk about it, and this is something that we have to teach our children: not to be bragging, not to say anything, that it is not good to be bragging about what they hold. It is important to be a humble person.

It is not only the children that should not brag. Adults and young adults that belong to the Mask or Rattler, or any other like the Cleansing of the House or being a Thi'tha. Being a Thi'tha, you don't brag about what you hold or what you can do. I was told that the things that I do belongs only to me and that I don't talk about it, I don't tell everybody. If people need help, then they will come to me and ask for the help. The people that belong to things like that should never have to be bragging about it and saying that they belong or they can do this or they can do other things. They know that they belong to it, and when people drink alcohol they should never, ever talk about any of the things that they belong to. My parents and grandparents used to talk about this, that people think that they have the courage to talk about things when they are drinking, and they used to say that this is the only time some people have the courage to speak is when they have alcohol in their mouth. But it is not the strength that they have; it is only because of the alcohol that they think they have the strength and then they speak openly about things. When they are drinking, they cannot discuss things about—or they get backward about discussing things. So they used to say that if you are a true person of being a Thi'tha, then you will just keep things to yourself, you don't talk about it.

Being a Thi'tha is very important, and the person who is one does not have to brag about what they know and what they can do. They just automatically do it when they are asked to do something. The power is very spiritual. The power is part of a prayer. The things that are used and the words are from our ancestors from way back, right from the beginning of time, and the words that have been passed on from one generation to another, and this is something that our Elders and our parents used to talk about. Words that were given were all in our Native language, Hul'q'umi'num'; it is not in English, it cannot be translated into English and it has to be learned in the Salish language. This is the most important part of our work: knowing it, hearing it, working at it and having the spiritual prayers that go with it is the most important part in our work. It is important to know all these things, and this is what I have passed on to my children and to my sisters. This came from my mother and her father and mother and her grandparents, and it was passed on down the line. It was all in the Salish language, not in English.

The spiritual healers of the cleansing and the verbal Thi'tha prayers are very important. They have to be memorized and the prayers are different. There is no translation in English for the Thi'tha prayers that are used; there are different prayers for different works. There is prayers for the plants that are used. There is prayers for the waters, the water that is used, and there is different prayers for the fire, for the cleansing of the home, for the spirits to go to the next world. There are many different ways of using the prayers in different kinds of cleansing. The cleansing of persons that have been bothered by spirits and the cleansing of persons that evil have been put onto, people that if someone puts evil words on them. Those are all different prayers that are used.

The children, the babies, they are never cleansed because they are still innocent and no harm should come to them, but if a child has been disturbed by a spirit, then they should be worked on by one of us. Oregon grape trees are used, ocean spray, and the consumption seeds, and water. The water is usually blessed, and the Oregon grape is also blessed. There is words for the blessing of the water, and there is words for the blessing of the Oregon grape. Ochre tumulh is used when the Oregon grape is blessed. These are all combined and used for cleansing a person, and similar things are used for someone who has had a stroke or to clean a home when a home is being spooked by a spirit or spirits.

Drying the Oregon grape is time consuming, and you have to know the number of branches to use for the household when our work is done. Everything is mostly in fours. Four bunches of branches and four bunches or four hands of Oregon grape for the people, four hands for the room itself or for where the casket was, and the same with bedrooms. Most everything always comes in fours in our Native community. Whether it is for us or for the Longhouse, the Masked Dancers, or the Rattler, for pictures, funerals, namings, and it can never be an odd number. It can be an even number but never an odd number.

All the things that are taught to us and are handed down have to be always the same, it cannot change. What was handed to my mother, what was handed to her, and she handed it to me or my brother and sisters, has to be handed down to the children, the same words, the same teachings. They all have to be as we received them, not different. We have to learn all the words, all the prayers, and it all has to be in our Native language, Hul'q'umi'num'. So this is what we have to teach our children and grandchildren.

Eight

YOUNG ADULTS have to remember that they cannot talk about this also when they are taking alcohol. They cannot be talking amongst themselves about it. If they want to talk about any of the teachings, they have to go to their Elder; they have to go their grandfather, grandmother, mother or dad. All the things that were taught to me and the ones that I am teaching my nephews, my nieces, my grandchildren, my sons and daughters, they have to learn it just as I did. They have to memorize everything just as I did: the teachings, the songs, the prayers, the shrubs that have to be used, the kind of ochre, the kind of seeds such as the q'uxmin consumption seed. The grease was used long time ago and it was deer grease that was used a long time ago. In place of that, Vaseline is used for mixing the ochre.

The ochre paint—there is usually someone that goes for the ochre paint. They are also taught where to find the paint. There are different people in the community that know where to get the ochre paint. The very red paint, the very bright red paint, we get that from the American people. People that are in Tulalip, and they bring it to us.

There are many different kinds of paints that is used for different purposes. For us, we use it when we have a cleansing after a funeral. We use the ochre on people's faces to show where they have cried. You put markings on their face for their tears, and this is washed off afterwards. It is washed off with water, but they never wash themselves. They can splash their face four times and wash off the paint, but they don't wipe their face. It is the person that is doing it that has to wipe their face. After the fourth time—the person's face is wiped four times—then they can do it themselves. They can wipe their own face. This is after the funeral that this is done, and only for a funeral or for someone who has been crying, or can't stop crying, and the tumulh is put on them and then washed.

I also use this when people are cleaning the graveyards. I put paint on them and I wash their faces. It is because of the sorrow of the people that have been gone a long time that I have to wash their faces, those that are working in the graveyard. A lot of the young men that were working in the graveyard were getting disturbed and they came to me to get cleansed. Some of the young men could not sleep, and some of the children and their grandchildren were getting disturbed, and they worried about it so they came over and asked for some help. I told them what I felt and I told them that they had to be washed, so I washed three of the people that came over. I washed their faces and brushed them off with my hands, with the water that was blessed, and I gave them the consumption seed to drink after I blessed the water. I had boiled some water, steeped the consumption seed and then I blessed it, let it cool, and then they drank it. This was for their own safety for them, so the spirits would just leave them alone, and that was part of the reason why they had to drink the consumption seed.

It is also for people that are attacked by spirits or ghosts. When a person is attacked by a spirit, and one side of their face or one side of their body will go numb or they will dribble on their mouth, then it is the consumption seed that is used on them. Their face and their bodies are brushed with the blessed water and the ocean spray and the consumption seed are used to brush them away, and then the consumption seed is steeped in boiling water for them to drink. This usually stops or get them better when their face goes numb or if they can't control their saliva anymore and they find themselves just dribbling. If a person like us will work on them, they will usually come out of it and they get better.

We are different from the one they call the shaman or Shne'um. The Shne'um is completely different from people that work as

Thi'tha or people that do the things that we do for people that lose their parents or become widowers. Bless their house with fire, work on the sharp things, the gun, and the needle and the paddle. These are the things that we do, and the Shne'um, the one that we call the shaman, is totally different. In this day and age there is no more shaman. The shaman used to help people and was able to cure many things. They used to do things that were supernatural things. They were very strong; they cured people; they were never evil.

The supernatural that my mother talked about was a contest that happened in Quamichan. It was eight different shamans. They put down eight buckets of water, eight rocks that were five, six inches long, they were kind of oblong, and this was just sort of a show or contest she said, to show that they could do certain things. So this was a gathering, a potlatch that was on down Quamichan, and this is what they did to show that they can do things. The eight buckets were put down full of water, the eight rocks were put in front of the bucket, and they were given a feather, each one of them were given a feather to put into the rock. She said that she thought that it would be impossible to do—to push a feather into a rock. The competition was that most of them did what was asked for, that they pushed the feather into the rock. Singing songs of prayer and pushing the feather right into the rock and then, after the feather was in the rock, setting the rock into the water, and then as the rock floated up, and my mother said that it danced in the bucket, it floated around in the bucket. It went around and around, just like it was dancing. She named only a couple, I couldn't even remember the names of the Shne'um that did all this, but this was in the early 1900s when this was done. She said that was the last of the very powerful shamans that used to be in Cowichan that did this. They were so powerful that they did curing and doing things like they just did with that rock. I did ask, "How did they do this? How did they become so powerful?" They became so powerful by staying in the forest for a whole year and receiving powers from different things in the forest.

There was only one old man that talked about it. When he went up to the mountain and he said that he was taking his bath, in one place that he took his bath, this was becoming a shaman; he took his bath, when he went into the water, he doesn't remember what happened. He said it was just like he became in a state of trance after he was in the water, and this was towards the end of the time that he was up the mountains for many months, had been up there already, and that he had gone into the water in this one lake. He remembers going into the water. He remembers diving and then when he was underwater it became like he was in a trance.

Somebody came up to him and asked him to follow, so he followed along, followed this person that was under the water. As he went deeper following that person, he came to a cave and went into this cave and then surfaced out of the water and came to a community. He said that there were people there. There were Old People that were already waiting for him, very old people, and they asked him what he had wanted. They asked him what he was looking for. When they asked him what he wanted, he wondered what they meant by what he had wanted. They told him without his answer, that they knew what he was looking for, but that he had to decide what he wanted. His answer was that he wanted to do good deeds for the people, and that was the answer they were asking for. They told him that if he had given the wrong answer, then they wouldn't let him, they would have just told him to go back where he came from; but he answered correctly, so he went in. They called him to go into another cave, go to their home as they called it: "Come into our home and you shall see. You can decide what you want and these are things that you will use to be able to help to do what you want, to do what you are asking for." They walked into this cave, and many things were shown to him, what he can use, and he said what really stood out for him, what he really saw when he was looking at all the things that were hanging up inside the cave, what really stood out was the bow and arrow, and he wondered what it was.

He was given an answer to his question without even asking the Old People. They told him that it was up to him what he wanted to do, but if he took the roots or the herbs then he would become a great healer; the bow and arrow, he would become a great hunter and so on. He thought about what he was doing. What he had wanted was for the people, so he took the roots and the plants that were there. That was his choice, and he became a good healer. He thanked the Old People, and they told him that he had to return to where he came from and that he received his gift. He started walking towards where he came from and then he said it seemed like he lost consciousness. When he woke up, he does not know how he got back to the shore of where he went into the water, but he had the plant in his hand and the roots in his hand. It was like proof to him that what he thought it became like a dream was truly real, and what he received was a gift. He completed his stay in the mountains by going for other baths, and this is how a shaman receives his power and how he gets gifts. He said that there was another world under the lakes where he received his gifts from. This is one of the shamans that my parents talked about; how they got their gifts.

There was one that I personally talked to that had gone up to the mountain and stayed up there for not a very long time. I can't remember if it was three or six months, and he always felt like he had not completed his "calling," as they called it. He talked about what happened to him while he was up in the mountains. He talked about what he did, the prayers he did, the work, the survival. How he had to survive. He didn't eat any food that was, as you call it, from the white man's world; what he ate was from the forest. He ate rabbits and deer, berries and everything that grew in the forest. That is what he said he ate, and he purified himself by going for his bath four times a day, early in the mornings, and going to four different places, not in the same place. He said he even went to the seawater, and when he went to the seawater, he remembers talking to a fish. I can't remember the name of this fish. I asked him "OK, what kind of fish is that?" and I remember him saying, he called it by name, and I thought it was a cod; no, it was not a cod. It had a big head but it wasn't very long. It was a big fish. "Is it some kind of a cod?" And he said, "No, it wasn't." Then he called it by the Indian name skw'e'. He was telling me, "Did you know that they are families too?" I said, "Yeah, I always thought they were living things." He said, "No, no, you are not listening." I said, "You mean that they are in a fish form but that they are human?" "Yes," that's what he said; this is true, that they spoke to him and communicated with him. He said that he went to other lakes and received gifts, but then he said that he had to come home too early so he said he felt that he never completed his stay up in the mountains. And I asked him, "What did you receive; what do you feel that you received?" All he said was that "Well, I can sense things, I know what happens to people, I can feel what happens to people, but I don't want to do anything about it because I never completed my training."

The three months that he stayed there was not long enough compared to others that stayed for the whole year and do the meditating—your meditating was the most important to do and the food that they ate from the forest, such as berries and rabbits, deer, grouse—there was special kind of herb potatoes that was used as potatoes. This was how the shaman became a great healer and the powers they received were given to them, the medication that they used, the different ways they became shaman. They received all kinds of powers from the forest, from the lakes, the meditations that they did, and they became powerful persons as helpers for the people. These are different: the shaman or Shne'um is different from the ones that practised the witchcraft. The witchcraft is very different. They practise bad things that when I inquired about it, I was told who they were and where they were, but I was told that was not needed. This was something that I didn't need to know or I shouldn't know about. But the Elders said that there is a need to know how to help yourself when bad things are thrown at you or if somebody puts bad words or if somebody uses bad words on you.

Nine

YOU KNOW, I have been asked by many of the young people what to do or how can you do it to help themselves. The best answer that my mother gave me was prayers. Prayers is the most powerful thing that can stop any evil. The evil that a person is using, and prayer is important to use.

The Natives, our People, used prayers all in our language when they go to the forest, and these are the same thing. They are prayers what we use when we take tree boughs for bathing, which is a cleansing. The cedar, the balsam—those are all for cleansing. And even for muscle strain and sprain or any kind of a wrist sprain. You can use the snowberry. Snowberry is really good to use. You take the snowberry bark, you scrape the bark off the snowberry tree and scrape it off as much as you can, almost a cupful. You boil that and then pick a cup of snowberry, and while the water is really hot, you bath your feet or put your ankle in the water and soak it. Then you just squeeze the juice from the snowberry and squeeze it into the water and rub it onto where the injury is. This cures it and numbs the pain, numbs the injury . . . that it doesn't hurt. I saw it used.

My dad used that on a new dancer who had injured a ligament and couldn't run. They said he was lazy because he couldn't run. They kept trying to make him run, and he couldn't hardly run, because he was limping bad. My dad really felt bad for him and felt sorry. He thought, well, there is something I can do for this young man. I can help him so he won't be abused by anyone. They think he is just pretending that he is injured, but he was really hurt. That is what he said to me. So he got this snowberry tree and scraped the bark and he scraped really lots, maybe more than a cupful. Then he boiled that and he got some snowberries. He told this young man, "You sit down and take all your gear off and put your feet in this small little tub." He had a small little tub and he stuck it in there and soaked it with the snowberries and squeezed the snowberries and applied it to the ligament. When that was done he told him, "Put your shoes on and try and stand up and see how it feels." The young man said, "It feels kind of numb." My dad said, "Yes, it should feel numb. That is what it does." He stood up on his right leg and said, "I don't feel the pain. I think it feels much better." So he was able to run that evening. He did that twice a day, in the morning and in the evening. And then everyone had just forgot that he was limping. He was running, and everyone forgot that he had an injury. Nobody asked what happened or whether he got better. This young man, he said he uses that. He has helped other people because he remembers what my dad did for him. He has told me that he has used it on other people. He said, "Your dad was a good man and he helped me, and so now I am helping other people by using that stuff that he used on me, the snowberry and the bark, and using it on people that have injuries and need to heal their injury, especially with ligament and muscle strain."

So there are ways of healing injuries with plants and herbs and with witchcraft that goes on. We have heard many people say that "There is something wrong with me, something was put on me or words were put on me," and when they come to me and say that, I just tell them that they should go and get a bath in the forest, which is the best way to get rid of it. To get rid of any bad words or anything that may have been put to a person. The balsam and the cedar and even sand can be used. You can apply the sand, rub yourself with the sand, and then go into the water. The same with the balsam or the cedar boughs, rubbing yourself with it, then after going into the water four times. That would have to be early hours of the morning. You have to do four mornings in a row for everything to come off of you. The Old People used to talk about what used to happen a long time ago, and this was all that they said, was taking a bath.

But there are other ways in the family that we can do by brushing them with branches and taking it off by blessing the branches with words which were given to us from the beginning of time. Which was given to my mother and then given to me, and we use it on the branches before we brush the people that come to us. The same with the people who become widows and widowers. When we work on people, work on the things that we are going to use on them, there are words that have been given to be used. It helps us and it helps a person for all those sharp things so they won't injure anyone else or themselves. That is the purpose of all the work that has to be done when they become orphans, widowers or widows.

The most important part is to know who to go to when a person thinks that there is something wrong. There are people in all the villages that can help; there are people that are practicing Shne'um, and there are the people that are the real Thi'tha, the Thi'tha which is the helper of the people. People that will help if there is something wrong that a person that called themselves Shne'um and does a wicked thing by letting something happen to a person. This is what the Old People used to say, that the person that does the bad things aren't really Shne'ums. They're only practising evil and they are not the real Shne'ums. They only know witchcraft, that do things to hurt other people. The real Shne'um is the one that helps the people, that cures, that knows what to do to help another person if there is something wrong, and they do sense things and know how to deal with things. But the person who practises witchcraft is an evil person and practises only the black, what the Old People used to call the black things in life, and do hurt people by doing something that will either injure them or they learn about hurting somebody by using pictures or figurines or things that like—those are the black, what the Old People used to call the black witchcraft or black Shne'um.

The real Shne'um doesn't do those things. They practise to help the people, to do the good deed, and they are the ones that know how to work with medicine right from the ground as herbs, and plants, roots, and they know how to do good things; and the Thi'tha, who is another helper of the people, like myself, and Ben Canute is also from the Thi'tha. There were many people from Thi'tha in the Cowichan reserve, Nanaimo, Chemainus Bay, and Saanich, Lekwammen, Songhees: they all had such people as Thi'tha—they knew how to help other people, knew how to deal with life in sorrow and many things. This is something that the people will have to remember, that there are different things in our lives and to know all these.

Ten

W HEN I WAS GROWING UP and going to school every day, my mother thought it was important for me to go school. My dad was always, he encouraged, he was the one that used to encourage me, but my mother was the one that insisted I go to school because she said she wasn't allowed by her dad to go to school, and she felt she missed a lot and she didn't want me to miss. She wanted me to learn to do writing and reading and do good in school. It seemed like it was always a busy, busy time, since that day we were doing—there was always something to do the whole year round.

Even though they were so busy, my dad still took the time out to go join the canoe paddlers because my grandfather had a canoe. He had built a canoe, and my dad and my uncle were always canoe pulling. Because they travelled in wagons in the earlier times, the late thirties, they didn't allow us to go along. It was only when it was local that we went along to the canoe races, but when they went to Esquimalt or Saanich or other places, they travelled on a wagon, horses and wagon. It took them two days going to places, and all I heard was, "You can't go along because there will be camping and starting early in the morning to get where they are going." They were usually gone for four or six days before they came home. Many times, there was a babysitter that was left with us.

And then the cars started to come into our lives. The first car that my dad had was a Durant. We felt that my dad really loved having an automobile, and that is where he learned how to drive and do things. That was in '39, 1939 when he had his first car. And then the travelling changed from wagons to cars.

If they weren't canoe pulling, then they were planting and seeding and working on the farm. So it was always something to do the year round. Wintertime, it was the dances that went on during the winter season. And then later on, we started to go across the States and strawberry picking and coming back in September to go back to school. So there was always something going on all year round.

But there was never a day that passed when my mother wouldn't be telling us about life, what was expected, what was going to happen in the future, and they used to say, "Well, you can't just marry anyone, you can't marry a hwunitum'." And I always thought, "Well, gee, I am only eleven years old, and she's talking about marriage." And then I started asking her how old she was, and then she started telling me that girls used to, weren't able to decide who they were going to marry; it was the parents that decided who they had to marry. Then she talked about her grandmother. Her grandfather was the chief of S'amun'a, Qihuletse', Chief Qihuletse'. When he got married he married an Indian princess who was a chief's daughter from North Van—Squamish, to be exact. Way up Squamish. They used to say Squamish was only twenty miles away from Mount Currie; that they could get to Mount Currie in just half a day by just walking across. So Qihuletse' married a princess, a chief's daughter from Squamish. This was exactly what was expected of me.

My father belonged to the Mask Dance on his mother's side. She belonged to the Mask Dance, the Raven. My mother belonged to the Mask Dancers but she was also a Thi'tha. She knew a lot, she had a lot; people had to come to her to ask advice. All the things that she learned from her parents she passed on to her children. She gave me all the knowledge that she had. She took me with her travelling to funerals and gatherings and she started telling me that I was going to have to, that she expected me to take over some day. I would have to start learning, start listening. And then I realized that I was listening to the same thing that she had said earlier in my life. Telling me all the things that were expected of me.

59

When I became fourteen, fifteen, then she realized I was going with someone, and then the background of the person wasn't suitable, and she told me why. She told me not to ever talk about it, but she gave me the reasons that I couldn't go with certain people. That I could not associate with them because of my status as a Thi'tha or because I was from the Mask Dancers. That I had to look for someone that had a nice background. When I met the children's father, when they found out that he took me home, and the discussion that went on and the deciding that I was to get married with the approval of the Elders as well.

As a child my playtime was very limited. I was allowed to go out and play with other children. Especially when they came to visit, I was allowed to go out and play with them. At school, because of the discipline, because of what she had said to me, I did not like to play softball, because of what she had said about laziness—that I was practising being lazy. So in school I played tag, but nothing else. I played with the little ones because I enjoyed their company. I sat on the swing and told them stories. They used to ask for stories, so I would tell them stories. I used to tell the stories in Indian but always in a hushed voice because the sisters were around. The children would encircle, and I would tell them stories, but away from the nuns where they couldn't hear, because if they heard me speaking Indian, the children and myself would have been punished. So it was always a hush-hush story that I told the children, the stories I was taught from my grandfather, my parents, my mother, my dad. When I got home from school, I would straighten up the house, then there was supper, because that became my chore. If I wasn't carding wool and teasing, carding, then I was getting supper ready and babysitting. My older brother babysat but not as much, as he had the responsibility of the wood to take care of, and while my dad was working, he had the chores of looking after the horses and cattle to be fed. So he had a lot of work to himself. He always covered that area. I was only allowed to do that chore if he wasn't around, but he was around most of the time, so I did all the work taking my mom's place in cooking because she was knitting.

Eleven

THEY HAD CIRCLES OF ELDERS, and I listened to them.
Listening to them, and now I realized this was happening for a
very good purpose. This was part of the training, to hear and listen to these Old People. Discussions that went on was for my purpose to hear. To know about the past, and having old man Wushq,
William Paul, who was a shaman, a Shne'um, and he was a great
person in his own lifetime. He was a very tender man; he was very
knowledgeable about a lot of things and he visited us very often.
He was there every day talking to us and telling us stories. These
were some things that were given to us as part of discipline. All
the stories were a part of discipline, part of being good and what
happens when you are bad, and they were all told in stories. There
were different stories for different times. There were stories that
were told to us when we were a bit younger to keep us from stray-
ing away from the house or going onto the road. To keep us from
going onto the road, they told us stories that we might be taken
away, and they talked about this giant woman who had a basket
of snakes, who had a great big basket with snakes in there, and
she stole children. And the children would listen to the story that
if they were bad and if they didn't listen, this woman would come
and steal them, and that they were going to be barbecued like a
salmon and pitch was going to be put on their eyes and then she
was a cannibal. She loved eating children, and she had her sister,
who was crippled—she was hunchbacked—who was a very good

person and the sister loved children; but the giantess hated children, she ate them. She would cook them, barbecue them and eat them. This is the kind of story that we were told so we would not wander from the house, we would not go very far. We were told that she was always looking for children, she looks for children in the evenings as soon as it is dusk, so it made us come in the house before it was dark.

That took important rules in our lives to keep us on our toes, not to be wandering away, not to go anywheres, but we were allowed to go swimming and different things as long as there was an older person to go with us, to look after us to make sure that we learned the time. We were taught how to tell time early in our lives by the shadow of the sun. Where the shadow goes and where it is when we are supposed to be. So we learned to tell the time by looking at our shadows and thinking and knowing what time and where we are supposed to be at certain times of the day. This was how we were taught discipline; we were told that we were on strict orders of doing things.

The boys, my brother, was also taught the same thing. The changes that came into our lives, puberty, and they told us what they could have done, what used to be done when the young lady changes into a woman. The Mask Dance that could have happened, but because of the hard times in '45 when the government had forbidden the potlatch and the Sxwuyxwi Masks, it didn't happen to me, but I am well aware of what they could have done.[1]

And this was about the time that potlatch was forbidden, the dances. The government was going after our people and saying we were spending too much money in the Longhouse. Some of our people were even imprisoned because they would not give up

---

[1] Ruby would have undergone the full traditional coming-of-age ceremony in around 1945 if the Potlatch Ban had not been in effect. The Potlatch Law (1884) banned participation in a potlatch ceremony involving gift giving, speeches and dancing. The following year, the government added an amendment which banned taking part in any Indigenous dance or ceremony. Items such as masks and regalia were seized and Big Houses torn down. In 1951 the Indian Act was amended and the Potlatch Ban lifted. See the Bill Reid Centre for Northwest Coast Studies, Simon Fraser University.

their Sxwuyxwi Mask: because they refused to give it up, they were imprisoned. A lot of our people went underground, and nobody knew who was who or who belonged to the Mask Dance because no one would talk about it. No one would say who belonged or who used it, or if they had any of that Mask Dance. It would be in secret and the place where nobody knew about it. This went on for a long time because of what the government was saying about that we were worshiping the devil and spending too much money.

Then they were taking it all away from us; they thought they were going to stop us so that we could learn faster, as they put it. Learn the white man's ways because we were the "wild Indians," as they called us. So they thought taking things away from us, our language, our Masks and anything that we did, and if they stopped us then we would learn faster. That's what they thought. They didn't want us to practise any of our Indian ways. They didn't want us to learn our Native ways so that children had to stop speaking Indian. By 1948, children were being punished. A lot of our children in residential schools that would sneak out and go to an Indian dance were getting punished. Even our day schools, if we went to the dance and were questioned about it, then we were punished for going to the dance.

Even the fish wars were starting. We weren't allowed to take so much fish anymore. We had weirs; they stopped the weirs. And they said, "We will give you the nets in place of the weirs. They will be better, if you use a fish net instead of using a weir." And our people believed that, what they were told, and they took the nets. Then after that, they went into, they changed that. Instead of having nets, they stopped the nets—we can't use the nets anymore—and gave us the dip nets. They again convinced us to use the dip nets; they believed that it was better for them to catch the fish with the dip nets. Then, this is after the dip nets, they started saying, "Well, you can go fishing only on certain days. You can't fish every day." They took the dip nets away and they started giving spears. We always used spears, but they said we could use only spears. It was getting harder for our people to catch the fish because they were closing it so many days a week. We could not fish every day. We tried getting the same amount that we used to have, having it ready for the winter. We used to have barrels of salted fish and a lot of fish smoked for the winter, and this wasn't happening anymore. Things were starting to change.

The war was the other thing that was really hard on us, when we had to—I think this was the German war, and they used to tell us that there might be bombs that will be coming around—and we had to make that sure our windows were closed and we had to cover our windows with blankets and blankets. Alec Canute used to come around, Chris Canute, then we would hear the siren right in Duncan. Then we'd hurry and close all the windows and cover it with blankets and make sure there was enough nails for the blankets so there wouldn't even be a spark of light from the house going outside. It was scary doing this. We wondered whether we will get bombed or not. We huddled and held one another because of the siren that was so scary.

The ration that we had to go through, the food we had to give up because of the soldiers that were around. We had only limited food; we had to have coupons that were for meat, for sugar, for butter, milk. We traded our milk coupons for something else that was needed. So it seems that there was one hardship after another. I remember the time we had to go without shoes. We had to save our shoes for school. We didn't mind, because it wasn't that hard to run around without your shoes. But they were hard times. I knew at times my mother went without food because she wanted us to eat, because there wasn't enough because of the changing times, things that were happening in our homes, the reserves. Life isn't easy, and this is what we were told. That's something mother always said: "Remember there's always hard times; you can always do something." That's one thing we were lucky for, having a farm and potatoes. She would take the potatoes and fry it for our meal. Mix it with salmon. She always had something to make it better.

Twelve

B Y THE TIME I was nine years old I had learned how to knit, to purl and the difference between the plain and the purl and the designs. Mother didn't have too much time of teaching me, so I learned from the sisters, learned how to knit. But once I learned the basic knitting, she started teaching me how to help her with the sweaters. She was always so busy making ends meet, and once I learned the knitting, then she started teaching me how to help her. The plain knitting or the purl and knit the bottom of the sweater. She had me make those for four or five of them, ready for her to knit a sweater. She would just count out how many stitches that I would have to make, whether it was round or for cardigan. Most of the time it was cardigans that she knitted and she traded either at the store or sold privately. She always seemed to get more money for the private sales because she got a lot of clothing that were brand new, and on top of that, she would get cash.

I did a lot of the carding, washing wool, teasing and carding. That was the first thing that we learned, was the teasing and the carding and then the knitting. I learned how to spin when I was about eleven. It was later on when I learned how to do spinning. It seemed like when I turned nine, ten years old, she started talking to me about becoming an adult, becoming a young lady, that my life was going to change. She was preparing me already at that age that there was going to be a change. Talking about changing into a woman and what I was going to have to do and what I was going to be doing, how I was going to handle that. "Being a woman," she said, "you have to have a lot of responsibility, to know when to get up, the right time to rest" that "going into adulthood, laziness isn't included. You can't be lazy." That we had to learn, that there is always things to do. She always said, "Look around when you get up, first thing you do is remember that people are going to look at you," and this is something that she said to me, "The first thing you do is look after yourself when you get up. Cleanliness, how you dress yourself, how you are going to look. It's going to be the same when you get married. Wash your face, clean yourself, take a bath and make sure your hair is done properly. Start the day off properly."

She said by being clean and doing your housework and looking after my father was the example. She was doing the knitting, and I had to take care of my dad. He had to be at work by catching a crummy[1] by six o'clock, or if he was logging close—he used to log for Evans Lumber Company—and he used to leave the house by seven o'clock in the morning, and I had to be up. By the time I was ten years old I knew how to make his lunch, fry eggs, making breakfast: fried potatoes and eggs and coffee or tea and sending him off to work. Mother had to be up early; she got up at five o'clock to do her knitting. She started on her knitting right away, and I did the lunch. Then I would get ready for school. I would do the dishes first, clean the kitchen and then get ready for school. By eight o'clock we were catching a bus, going to school. So by the time I was ten years old I knew what to do that was my everyday work, what I had to do every day, and I was being prepared to enter womanhood.

I was told what was going to happen. She always said you either have your change from your childhood to adulthood, thirteen or fifteen, thirteen, fourteen or fifteen. She said she always said there were not too many girls that will have a change at fifteen; it was usually thirteen. The preparation time for adulthood was all that, how to look after the family, the training of household chores. What I did when I get home from schools because she was always busy so I had to make the supper. By the time I was eleven years

---

1 A vehicle used to transport logging crews.

old I was doing breakfast and supper. My dad was bringing money in, but he was paying for the tractor and the car. He always had an automobile. And my mother always knitted to make ends meet by buying groceries for the house.

Every June we would leave school early. By June 11, we were pulled out school and we would go across the States to pick berries. My dad would stay home and he would continue logging, but my mother and myself, my brother, my younger sisters would go to Mount Vernon and pick berries. This was another different kind of life we had there. Getting up early in the morning. She would always prepare first for the time we would go berry picking. She would get a sack of potatoes and basic things that are needed, like flour, canned things that she can use for cooking, like corned beef, and she usually always had soup, vegetable Campbell's soup, and smoked salmon. The dried fish, smoked salmon, she always took it with her. When we cooked that we always scraped it where it's open and then soak it in water and that was used, it would be boiled for a meal. The work was very intense, very hard. We had to work from daybreak, which mean we never had any breakfast. We would just get up and go and pick berries. Then by ten o'clock we would have something to eat. Then twelve o'clock, we would either go down to the camp and have soup, or else if we're far from the camp, then she would have sandwiches for us. Summertime is a hard time to be picking berries. We would pick until three o'clock, and then the bosses would say there was no more picking because it was too hot, or if it was raining then that was another reason not to pick in the afternoon. It was really hard, but we always seemed to be trying to do better than the day before. This is always what she would say before we go off to work: "Let's try do it a bit better than yesterday!" If we picked ninety crates, which would be ninety dollars for that day, then she would say, "Let's try to make it to a hundred dollars today." So we always had a goal to try and make in one day. But there was always a reason for picking. She was always saving the money that we picked for. She always counted it and made sure there was a goal for what we were doing.

By the end of the strawberries we would have made maybe $600, $800 for the strawberry season. Then we would go to pick currants. With the money we made during the currants, she bought school clothes and things like that and shoes that are going to be used for the year. Then we would go raspberry picking, then that money would be put aside for something that they needed in equipment. The first one we worked for was a tractor. That was we made about $2,000 that year right to the end of the season, right from strawberries, currants, raspberries, blackberry, hops, and each place we went to was about three or four weeks during June, July, August, September, and we'd come home in October.

We would miss some school days. We always stayed there to make it to the goal that they needed for whatever they needed for equipment. Like a disk or harrow or something that goes with the tractor. Other years that we were going and worked for a car, just for a down payment for a car. So there was always something that had to be, that we worked for. She said what you worked for would show you what you worked for, by paying for something that you know we will have for all of us, not just for one person. It was for the whole family. It was just like we were being trained for something, to know the work you have to do to earn money, where to put it, what to do with it, to understand what life is about.

When we came home by October, we were back to same thing that we were doing before. Knitting, carding, teasing, washing wool. Then after the learning of the knitting—it was much later—I was about twelve or thirteen by the time I learned how to spin. She worried about the wasting of wool. If I was going to make a mess and waste all the wool by breaking it and everything else. But I watched her very closely when she spun, and she was a real fast spinner, and how she spun the wool. So when I started spinning I just copied how she spun the wool, and I was surprised that I caught on the first day I worked on spinning of wool. Just by copying how she did it and what she did. She always stretched her wool so that it was so even, and I tried the same thing, and to my surprise that is what is exactly what happened to my wool: it was all even and really fine, the ways she spun her wool, it was fine not rough. Then she started letting me do all the spinning after she realized I was spinning just like the way she spun her wool.

Old art revived

Cecilia Alphonse, teaching basket weaving to her student shows her all the basic stitches.

Newspaper clipping of Ruby's mother Cecilia teaching weaving.
Courtesy of Molly Peter. Photographer unknown, late 1960s.

I always took her as a woman who was pushing for perfection. Everything had to be perfect. She didn't like anything to be out of place, even the house, the kitchen, and she always said to us girls, especially me, "There is a place for everything and that you cannot have something out of place, and your work when you work or spin, it should be perfect, it shouldn't be rough. Don't think that you can show off something that is roughly made. Remember, you have to be proud of your work. It should look at its best."

Thirteen

EVEN AT THE AGE OF TEN we already knew the "where you are not supposed to be touched by any man or boy," and she would always say, "Do not let any man touch you like this. Do not let a boy touch you like, put his hands over like this," and she would touch me where a boy is not supposed to touch or a man. These were how we were told the warnings that were told about the don't touch, bad places that a man should never be touching, a man or a boy. We were made aware that not to talk to strangers, and even we were told we are related to a lot of people, but we were told that we should not ever be too friendly with a man or a boy, whether that's related, even though we are related, maybe that man or boy will have a different idea about you as a girl.

We used to run to our grandparents, Alphonse George, they were in Quamichan, and we were at Lakes Road. We used to run, bring milk to them or butter, and that would be two miles. They would give us a half a bucket of milk or two or three pounds of butter to bring to our grandparents for their use. But before we left, there was always that warning: "You be careful when you go, you watch out. If you are a girl, and if a man or a boy promises money or anything like that or asks you to go do something, come and do this, don't listen, you either start running or start screaming if you are touched," and that is how we were warned about bad touches. I was about ten when I was allowed to bring something to my grandparents, delivering butter, eggs and milk and coming home again.

Sometimes I used to go with my late sister, who used to visit us. My dad was previously married to Margaret Canute, and I had an older sister that I was really attached to, Adeline, my older sister. She was my half-sister. When she visited with us, she stayed with us when she was a teenager, and we used to go together and deliver butter and milk and eggs to our grandparents together. But I knew I was told her mother was different. She had a different mother, and when we got to our grandparents and grandma decided to send some butter to Comiaken. And I didn't know what that meant, I just thought that we were going next door. I didn't know where Comiaken was and I thought that we were just going to go a little ways, but we went quite a ways and we went another two miles, and this was the first time I met my stepmother. And she was very nice. I didn't tell my mother about her. I was introduced to her by my sister and, apparently, she had had another daughter. When she called and she told me to sit on her lap and she was telling me, "Oh my gosh, you are just a replica of my other daughter that passed away." I didn't know that she had, that there was another daughter, that there would have been another half-sister, but I guess that one died. We came back home and then my sister told me, "Don't tell your mom, or we will get into trouble," so I didn't tell. I didn't want my sister to get into trouble.

It was not only the girl that was warned about behaviours of people, about sex abuse. It was even little boys, even my brother was warned about it, and it was much later on in the years before I found out why she was so afraid, so scared of things happening to us, the experience that she went through, not herself, or what she saw happened that made her very aware of abuse, sexual abuse. Her nephew had died of being abused, and this made her very much scared for her own children. The little boy that was sexually abused by an older, by a young man, and the baby, the child, died. He was only four years old, and this was before there was police or law that it could be reported to, but it actually happened, and that made her very afraid for her children or for any of the children that she was responsible for. It seemed that as soon as I turned seven, after the age of seven, it was always my mother that talked about life and told stories about how the young ladies conducted themselves in public. She always wanted us to play only with girls, and the boys play with boys. She said, a long time ago they never used to be allowed to mix, the children with boys and girls. The fathers are the ones responsible for teaching the boys about life, and she said it was her responsibility to give us, to tell us what we have to do; and she, from the time of seven years old, it seems like there was a story that went with a reason not to talk to strangers.

There was one story that she always gave us, was the young lady with thirteen brothers. And she was from a big family of all boys and one girl, and she was sequestered from everyone when she turned into a young lady. And she used to go for her walks, daily walks for exercise, and she would walk down to the beach and back. And she would meet this young man that was chewing gum. The first day she didn't talk to him, and then the next day she saw him again, and it was until the fourth day that she asked him where he got his gum from and if he would share some gum with her. The young man told her that the gum was not very far from where they were; it was just down the beach, and that he was going to show her where it was and to follow. With all the warnings this young lady had, she still followed him and went down to the beach. When they got down to the beach, there was a little canoe there that was called ho'tum'e, and he told her that the gum wasn't there, but it was across the river, on the little island across the river, and to get on this canoe, and he promised that he was going to bring her back after as soon as he got the gum for her. She believed him and she got on this canoe, and it went across to this island. When he got to the island, she got off and followed him, and the place where she was brought to was made of ice, the front part of the house was all ice. She went sliding and went into this house and she asked for the gum, and he gave her some, but he said she was not going to be allowed to leave again. She became a prisoner in this place, this young man's place, and this man took her as his wife against her will, without the family's permission or without asking for her hand, and she became a prisoner.

It wasn't until late in the evening that the brothers started worrying about their sister and went looking for their sister and went looking down to the beach, and found frills from her shawl were on branches leading to the beach. And they found a canoe at this beach, so they crossed and went across to this island. But when the first brother got there, he just found that this house had a sheet of ice in front of it and he was sliding around on it, going into this place, as he reached the house, knocked and was let in; but this man killed him. Her brother was killed by this young man, and laid him down on the ice and covered him up.

This was one of the favourite stories that my mother told us, that all the brothers of this young lady were killed, all twelve of them. Each one of them went looking for their sister and each brother was killed and laid on the ice and covered up. They were all lined up, lying on the sheet of ice, and the mother cried and cried. She cried for three days, and as she was crying, her nose was dripping down snot, and it was piling up, and then she kind of noticed that there was something happening to the snot below her where she was crying into. It started to take form, forming into a human being, and it was happening quite quickly. In a matter of time, it started, it grew into a human form and then this child that came from that became human, from that snot, started talking to her, asking why she was crying and asking her to stop crying. And then she told him that he, there was a daughter that went missing, that her twelve boys all went missing too when they went looking for their sister. And then this boy just started turning into a young man, and he told his mother, started calling her mother and telling her that he was going to go and look for his brothers and his sister.

So she showed him where the brothers had gone, where they went to cross on the canoe. He also went across and getting to the place where the man Skwathshun' lived. He found the front yard was all a sheet of ice and he went to the house. He brought a knife along with him and a staff, and when the door opened, after his knock, this Skwathshun' answered and asked what he had wanted. And he said, "I came for my sister." And he asked, "Where are my brothers?" And he was told, "Your brothers are all lying down outside, they are covered up, they are all dead." This Skwathshun' said, "Well, and you are going to die too."

He was going to kill him, but the young man got the best of him and killed him with the staff-spear, and then he saved his sister. He opened this Skwathshun', opened him up, and he found all the hearts of his brothers inside him. And he took each heart and put it back into each brother and closed them up, and he saved all his brothers; they all came back to life. Skwathshun' had swallowed all the hearts in one piece, and did not chew it, so they were all in one piece; and he was able to put it all back into the brothers' chests. He took his sister home and all his brothers with him back across to his mother. And then they went home, and the next day, they decided they were going to go hunting. They were going to hunt for some food, and that youngest brother had been questioning his mother where this other young man came from, where did this new brother come from. She kept saying, "I am not going to tell you," but he kept pressuring and asking and asking, and then, finally, she told this youngest one the truth about the youngest brother: that when she was crying, that the snot that was falling from her formed into human and became their brother. When they went hunting, they all got on a canoe and went together, and the youngest brother starting making fun of this brother, he started telling his brothers about their youngest brother, that he was nothing but a snot, and it upset the younger brother at what was being said about him. He didn't say anything; they just went hunting together.

Many of the brothers didn't catch anything, but the youngest one caught deer and elk, and they came back to the canoe and they were going to bring back their catch to their mother for a feast. And on their way home, the younger brother was again making fun of this new brother, new younger brother, of what he was, and telling his brothers. The oldest brother kept telling him to be quiet, that they were saved by this younger brother, but that one brother kept on making fun of this snot man. When they got home, they got off the canoe and started to bring their catch in. He told his brothers, "You bring my catch to your mother and prepare it, and I will stay on here. I want to sit on the canoe for awhile." So they just left him there and they went in and prepared the food, prepared the catch they had, cooked it and got it ready for the feast.

Then the mother asked, "Where is your brother, where is your new youngest brother?" And the older brother was telling them that the youngest of them was picking on him. He was making fun of him, and that they were stopping him, and he wouldn't stop talking, saying things, he was saying bad things about our brother, our new brother. "He is on the canoe." So they asked the oldest brother, "Go and call your brother, tell him to come in here. I want him in here with us. He saved you." That is what the mother said to the oldest brother. "Go call him, ask him to come and join us. We are going to have a feast, and I am just happy that you are all here." So the older brother went out. When he got to the canoe he couldn't find his brother and he called out to his mother that his brother wasn't on the canoe anymore. She came running down, and when she pulled the blanket off where he was sitting, he had just disappeared. All they found was the snot that was at the back of the canoe. Because of all the name-calling and abuse language that was being used, he had turned himself back into snot; he disappeared and turned into snot again.

This was one of the stories that we were told. A story for us to remember that we should not abuse our siblings, brothers and sisters, or for girls to not be wandering away and not follow any one person who is offering any candies or any kind of goodies. I found that very effective to me and my sisters because it did help me when I was about nine years old; and this story was told to us quite often, and we were told about not to follow anyone that would offer any goodies or money. And we were often sent down to Quamichan to our grandparents to deliver butter or eggs or milk, and sometimes I went by myself, and this one time that I was going down to Quamichan to deliver things to my grandparents, and she always said, "If you are carrying anything heavy you just drop it and run if anybody does anything or you get scared."

I was walking to Quamichan to deliver some butter, and there was a shortcut. There was a trail going into the reserve, just after the bridge there is a little field, then this young man that was coming. I was about nine, and he was about seventeen, and I knew him, but I was always remembering my mother's words. And he was saying to me, "I have got something for you." He said, "Come here, I will show you I have some money for you," and I asked him what he was talking about and I kept on walking away, and he said, "Come here, come back here, I will give you some money and I have some things for you. I will show you." I was about six or eight feet away from him and there was a fork in the road. He was going toward the field, and I was on this road and I started running, and I was so scared. And it was the words of my mother that I had remembered and the story that was told to me about what can happen. That young ladies can be abused and we can get hurt, so I ran all the way to my grandparents' place. And when I got there I was really shaking and scared, and it wasn't my grandmother that noticed, it was my grandfather asked me what was the matter. And instead of telling him I just sort of closed up and I couldn't talk for a long time. And then after I told my grandmother, it seemed more right to talk to my grandmother and tell her. But instead, my grandmother got angry at me for a reason I don't know. She started getting mad, and I can't even remember what she said, and my grandfather came to my defence and he said, "She is not going to walk home by herself." And my grandmother stopped getting angry because he said he was going to walk me home, "She is not going to walk home by herself. I am going to walk her home." And he told her to leave me alone. I don't even remember what my grandmother was saying to me; all I remember was that she was angry, and my grandfather brought me home.

But telling stories to children and examples of what can happen to them is very important. And if it wasn't for the stories I was told, I probably would have been tempted and wondered what that man was going to give me or how much money he was going to give me, because he kept talking about money and that he had some things for me. But because of the stories and maybe all the warnings that my mother kept saying to me helped and I just ran away.

Fourteen

T HE TEACHING that she was giving us started changing when I was nine, about the age of nine, and she started talking about my life, what it is going to be, the importance of marriage, of having only one mate for a lifetime, and I used to tell her that I was not ever going to get married. She used to laugh at me and say, "Well, I said the same thing as a child and look at me I have you, and you are going to have children, too."

By this time two of her nieces got married. Rose Johnnie married Victor Johnnie, and she had quite a few children. She has two children left. She passed away in '76. And Tillie died, her youngest sister died when she was just not too, oh, she married. The first marriage she had, she had three or four babies, and they all died before they reached the age of two. I don't know what the reason was, but her husband died of TB, and then she was single. She came home to Mom for about two years and then she married somebody else. She had two boys with Spike Henry, and there's only one boy that survived, and he had two children, so Tillie had two grandchildren from the second marriage. The youngest one that she was raising, she had left Mom and ran away to Kuper Island. She came home and then she stayed with her other grandparents on her dad's side. And then later on, she got together with someone from Westholme. She had one child from that man, and that baby died at the age of two of pneumonia; and then she had another marriage and had children, about five children, and two with another man. Mother tried to keep her nieces, keep in contact with them, but they kind of drew away from her once they got married and then kind of lost touch. One moved away to the States and lost contact with her for some time.

And then she always told me that when I get married, "You are going to have to remember who you are coming from." I always asked her, "Why? What do you mean by who I am coming from?" And she used to talk about how the people used to know other people by their status of what they hold, and which ones had the higher status and the lower status. And I never, never could grasp it, I couldn't understand what she meant until it was just before I got married, and then I realized what she was talking about. But this is what she was always telling me when I was about ten, eleven. I had to watch myself—you can't marry just anybody. "You'll have to remember who you are and what you hold," and I didn't realize at the time at the age of ten that there was so many things that she held. I used to follow her, I used to go everywhere with her, I saw what she did, but I thought that was just normal. I thought everybody, I thought the whole Cowichan Valley did the same thing, but that wasn't so. It wasn't the whole Cowichan Valley. It was only certain people.

My brother was also being trained, being lectured, but it wasn't by my mother. My mother did only part of it; then she said Dad had to do the rest. He had to talk to his son, do his part in talking to his son, because my brother will be having a change of ways and he was already thirteen, and they were saying that it was kind of late; but he was being prepared by both parents and grandparents. I just remember when it did happen, my dad taking him for a bath and my grandfather being there, and I only heard parts of it, and it was later on I was told what it was, what he had to do. So he wouldn't be lazy or he wouldn't lose his teeth, he had to roll some rocks inside his mouth, a small pebble, a certain kind of pebble, and just roll it. I can't remember whether it was one or two pebbles. They were very tiny, but he rolled it, and it was to keep the teeth from deteriorating and it would straighten it out if it was crooked. I know he went for his bath and the other thing was looking for a flat rock, that's from the one called kw'unt'als[1] and that's used for a young boy when he has a change of voice entering manhood. They take this flat rock and rub it on his chest so he would not have breasts, so he would have a flat chest.

We were told it was only for a man, and a girl cannot use it. But I know of a girl that did use it, and we had discussed it, and because of the joke that Mother used to say and she used to tell young girls that "if you don't watch out you are going to have to throw your breast over your shoulder because it was going to grow real long." I used to tell my mother to stop telling these dirty jokes, I called it a dirty joke, and she thought it was really funny that she was telling these young ladies stories like that their breasts were going to grow long and heavy and end up throwing it over their shoulder. She used to demonstrate; she didn't just say it, she demonstrated what they were going to be doing. But she was telling this to pre-teens, eleven and twelve years old.

And then it did happen to a couple of girls that had changed, that were changing their life into womanhood during puberty. And they went for a bath up in the mountain, and I went along with them to show them where to go and help them out with my mother. And my mother stayed ashore and she told me, "You go along with them." But the girls were ahead of me, and I didn't know and I didn't know what they were up and I didn't think of anything of what they were doing. I just thought they were just going to be going into the water after the work that was done to them using branches and sand, things like that, like you use sand on your body so the hair won't be growing all over, and you also use branches of balsam, rub it on your body after, before you go into the water. And the girls followed their instructions, and I helped them, and then they were going into the water, and I didn't notice what they had picked up while they were walking. They knew, they must have planned it or something, but it wasn't until I saw what they were doing and it was already done by the time I really noticed. They had picked up these two flat rocks and they had rubbed it on their breast, and I screamed to stop them, but

---

1 The English name is basalt.

it was already too late. It was already done by the time I realized what was happening, but that had kind of proved that what the Old People had said about the purpose of that rock, the purpose of doing that. It showed up later when she got married and had a baby: she couldn't get very much milk for her baby. Both girls were like that: they couldn't get very much milk in their breast for their baby. So it did show up later that it was true what the Old People were saying, that it was only for a boy and not for girls.

My brother did all of this when he had his change of life, changing into man, and his voice was changing; he used that rock also and he used the sand on his body so he wouldn't have any hair on his body, and he also used the balsam or cedar. Either balsam or cedar are the same. Cedar are mostly for boys. The sand, rubbing sand on your body to keep from getting hair is true, and that is why, that's the purpose of using sand—so you won't be hairy and growing hair all over your body. Notice that there is hair on a lot of men's bodies, and Native People they don't, but they take care of themselves. They have someone look after the boys when they change into a man, and this is, I think most Indians know this. A lot of them have different other ways working, doing things with changing life. Mother used to tell us, "Our teachings are only for us. We cannot apply to another Indian Nation or any another, like people from Saanich or Nanaimo, and tell them this is the right way, because they have their own ways: there are different ways of doing things among the Natives." Even when we go to Vancouver, Musqueam, Merritt, Kamloops, they do things differently; there are other ways of doing things. It's always not the same. It's similar but not the same.

My dad and my brother used to do a lot of hunting. We used to drop them off at Maple Bay. There was a road there, just before or about two miles from Maple Bay, and we used to turn into this dirt road and drop them off. They would walk across and come out at St. Ann's, and they always had one deer or two deer. My dad was a very busy person, and it was only during the weekends and he used to like to hunt or fish and he used to go hunting. We were never without food. There was always something for the table. Then my older sister got married and she used to bring some food, her husband used to bring food over to us—bring fish, most of the time it was fish she used to bring over. She used to come and help us with work.

She was the last person that was ever proposed to the Indian way. She was raised by my grandparents after my dad and his first wife separated, and my grandparents raised my sister. And I was very close to her. She was a very tender person, quiet spoken, and she went to school at St. Catherine's. And she was about the last person that was proposed to the old way. She was raised by my grandparents, and because they were elderly, the people that asked for her hand decided to do it the old way. So the grandfather and the parents and other people came to ask for her hand. I remember my grandparents getting to my dad and asking him what he thought of the proposal. And my dad, his only comment was that the people were respectable people and he couldn't say, because he didn't raise his daughter; and he left it up to his parents to care of, to decide what they were going to do with their granddaughter, whether they were going to accept or not. My sister was only fifteen at the time. She wasn't allowed to decide or allowed to speak out whether she wanted to marry this young man or not. She knew him by sight because she had seen him during the strawberries-picking times and different functions, but she wasn't friendly with him. He was a respectable person as far as she thought, a nice-looking man. And my dad didn't know what to do, and he decided because he didn't raise his daughter, and my grandparents had decided that they were going to give her away to these people. The young man sat outside my grandparents' place for two days without eating. It was frustrating my grandmother because she knew the young man never ate, that he was starving; that's what was worrying her. My grandfather was determined not to answer right away. His concern was that it was going to be a lifetime for his granddaughter, and it was more his decision than my grandmother's. He was the one that decided to accept after the second day. It was later on in the evening by the time he decided to give his granddaughter away to these people, and invited them into the house. Not the young man—the parents were invited into the house to accept the marriage proposal. So the parents of this young man came in and then they were given the answer of the proposal that they were—that my grandfather had decided to give his granddaughter away to them.

And then my grandmother started fussing around about it after the decision was made. She started trying to decide that she was against it, but my grandfather had already made the decision, but she was fussing about giving her granddaughter away. It wasn't until the second afternoon by the time she was taken away, the proposal was accepted and then after it was accepted, the young man was invited in. The food that they brought was accepted, and they were cooked and the meal was made for them. There was a feast after; then my sister was taken away to live with these people. But my grandfather's decision—when he decided, he told them his granddaughter had to get married, that if they were going to marry the Indian way there had to be another marriage by the church. This was another stipulation he made, so it wasn't only an Indian wedding, but it was also a Catholic Church wedding. They were legally married after three weeks later and they got married by the church. She had eight children with this man, and then their marriage broke up, and she went with another man of whom she had three children with, so there were eleven children altogether. But it was after the second marriage and we discovered she had leukemia, and she died of cancer, leukemia. My sister had a lot to do with my life. She sort of set example of how, what happens as a young woman. By the time she got married I was about fourteen and I was already having to do with a lot of things.

Fifteen

BECAUSE I WAS ONLY eleven or twelve years old when I started working on the tractor—plowing, disking, harrowing, seeding. This is all during the spring. Going to school was a very important role. The hard times that we had in school about the language; but it seemed like that our parents seemed to have set their lives into trying to have us work, trying to better with our lives in both worlds, in the white society and in our Indian ways. By the time I was a teenager, a lot of things had come back, things that went underground, like potlatches that they used to have that was forbidden, that we couldn't have the Indian dances, and our language that was forbidden, that we were getting punished for. It seemed that a lot of our people, the parents that came out of residential school—a lot of the parents, a lot of the people that were in residential school were away from home for seven to eight years from nine until they were sixteen. Some of them didn't come home until they were sixteen years old. Some of them left at seven years old and they never made it home until they were eleven, twelve years old. There were many reasons for that happening. Like one person that, persons that I knew, they never came out of residential school from the time they left at seven and eight years old, and they never came out until they were twelve and thirteen years old. This was just an example of young people being sent away, and the mother didn't have no way of keeping them home and she just left her children there—in residential school. Then when they came out, they only understood part of their language. They didn't speak it at all, and this happened to a lot of the people. They didn't get to learn the teachings. People that were from the Mask Dance Sxwuyxwi that were left in residential school, they didn't get the teachings about the Sxwuyxwi and the Longhouse and their own teachings about raising families. This was lost, completely lost from these young people that were in residential school.

And there were many of them. I know my dad went to residential school, but he was only there for three years and he came home. But the ones that from 1940 to 1948, a lot of them stayed there for many, many years and a lot of them came home when they were sixteen years old. Some of them couldn't even speak their language or some of them just understood their language. They just totally lost their culture and the teachings, how to raise children, how to take care of themselves, how to keep from temptation, and even the cultural things like the Sxwuyxwi Mask Dance and the Rattler. A lot of them lost this altogether. Some of the people lost their Masks. That was taken away from them. At one point, I remember one person being imprisoned because they wouldn't let go of their Mask, and that was earlier. That was in about 1935. The young people that were in residential school lost a lot, and even to this day, they can't seem to grasp, they don't know what happened to them. They can't even realize, they can't even grasp what is wrong or how it happened. The people that have come up and are trying to help themselves are those that have participated in the Longhouse, just recently over the past ten to twenty years. They have been participating and they are starting to grasp a lot of the teachings from going to the Longhouse during the winter. This had a made a lot of difference with our Native People, and even the young people are starting to realize this. My brother, who was taken as a dancer at the age of sixteen and he was initiated into the Longhouse, but he was never in residential school. I was never in residential school. I had no idea what had happened in the residential schools. It was much later before I found out what had happened. What was happening. It wasn't 'til after I got married that I heard a lot of things about the residential school.

When I was fourteen or fifteen and did all the work helping my father with the farm, my brother left home for some time at the age of sixteen, and he left home. He came home for a short while when he was initiated and then he left again. My parents felt bad, but they seemed to have turned to me to become their helper around the farm, and I did a lot of work with the tractor. Doing the plowing and helping my dad. All the things my brother used to do, I had to take over. I had learned how to start the tractor. My brother showed me what to do, so it wasn't hard to do the things that he was doing. I was happy to be able to help my parents, my dad, with the work.

With all the work that I was doing, I still had to keep up my education. This was something, my mother was determined for me not to fail in my education. My studies and my school work were very important. I guess the reason she was so determined to have me go to school because she was denied. Her father was very, very old fashioned and he didn't want his daughter to be in the public or to leave home to go to school. When that happened, she wanted me to be the one to succeed in education in all the things that she missed. She wanted me to be able to read and write and be successful in any of the school work that I did. So even with the work I did with the farm, she still made sure I went to school, that I did my studies, that my school work was one hundred per cent. She always asked about what I was doing, even though she didn't understand what it meant. She didn't know how to read. She didn't know how to—all she asked was if I did good and how good, what was the best I was doing. Was I on top of the class?

I always told her that they always had us competing in the classes: with math and English, spelling tests, and there was three girls, four girls, that were in competition from grade three to grade seven. That was Lily, myself, Cecilia, and Edith, and we had to compete with one another with all the work we did in math. All the tests that we did, we competed. English and spelling tests: we had to be one hundred per cent spellers to be able to compete with other classes. So that is how she kept up, how she made sure I was on top of my class. She always asked about what I was doing and made sure that I was doing my work.

It wasn't only school that was important. The teachings, it was repetition; and I was always reminded constantly who we are and the things that we have to remember as an Indian person. We were constantly told, "Don't forget that you are an Indian, you are Thi'tha," that there are teachings that you have to follow, that you have to. She used to say, "The repetition that comes with teaching. You have heard it before, you've heard it many times and don't ever say you have heard it already." You just agree with what you are being told. You never, ever say, "I heard it already." You can never say that about the teachings, no matter how many times you hear it. You still listen to it and you remember what you are being told. So from the time I was little and the changes that came with it at certain ages, from infant to child to your puberty, and then puberty time, young adult—these are all changes that were happening and constantly reminded that we could not answer back that "you already said it to me." You can't say that. No matter who talks to you, no matter who tells you, you don't ever say that you already heard it from someone.

Changes, the times and preparation for adulthood. Marriage, the teachings of what is going to happen—this was always stressed how we were going to be and what we were going to do, and there was always examples of what can happen if we got married and lived with our in-laws. She said, "OK, suppose if you got married and you ended up living with your in-laws: you are not going to ever be able to think for yourself, you are going to have to be an obedient person and listen to your in-laws because you are not going to be able to decide on things yourself, because that is the way it is when you live with your in-laws." And she said, "Well, I am an example of that. I lived with my in-laws. I had to take care of my mother-in-law, I had to cook for her, clean up their rooms, doing the laundry. Everything was done the way the mother-in-law wanted, that's how it is when you are with an in-law. You do it the way they want things, not the way you see it. You have to obey your in-laws. Whatever they decide, it is their decision, not yours, because you are living with them." She always said, "You cannot ever answer back to any Elders when you are living at your in-laws' home." She always said, "When you get married you are not going to be like the way I was, because that was a hard life, and I always had to be obedient to my in-laws. Everything was decided for me. The cooking, the time of sleep, the time to get up, the time to cook for her son, who is my husband, and what to cook for supper, and even the shopping that was done." She had to follow what was decided for her. She told me it was not a happy life to be living with in-laws. She said she wasn't happy.

She was only fourteen years old when she was given away and she lived with her in-laws for ten years, and she said she was really never very satisfied. She had to follow everything, and then later on, she was abused by her alcoholic spouse. The husband went into taking alcohol so much and abused it, and she said that she didn't want that happening to any of her children. So she more or less decided earlier that she didn't want me to marry and be living with in-laws. I didn't understand what she meant by this; by saying that I was fourteen and she was telling me all this, and I thought, "I didn't know what she meant by not wanting me to live with my in-laws, because I wasn't thinking of getting married." And I told her, and then she just said, "Maybe you are saying that now, but you will be saying something different later. But I want you to remember what I am saying. I am telling you I don't want you getting married and living with your in-laws." Later on, she started talking about how I had to be careful of who I was going to go with or go out with. She was always afraid that I might just marry, go with someone that they didn't know, my parents and grandparents. And I couldn't understand what that meant. I didn't know what she meant by you just can't marry just anyone. I couldn't understand because why was I to be careful, why was it not just anyone, what did that mean? I didn't realize that not all people carried what we carry from, like the Rattler, the Rattler or being a Thi'tha.

She often said, "You have to be careful of who you go with," and I kept wondering why. It was much later on before I found out, before I really realized I was told about it, but I didn't realize what it meant. Her grandfather Quyxuletse' was a chief. Quyxuletse's wife was a princess from Squamish. She was a daughter of a chief and she was proposed to and brought from Squamish. It never dawned on me that this made a difference, not only the things that we had, what we held, but that we were from descendants of chiefs from Squamish, USA, and Cowichan. She kept telling me, and I didn't really realize this. I listened, when I was allowed to go out to a carnival. The warning was always there—be careful of who you talk to, be careful of who you associate with when you are alone.

I was about fifteen when I was allowed to go to a carnival with my younger sister and my cousin Catherine Joe and Theresa Alphonse. My parents reluctantly let us go to this carnival, and I think we were timed as to how long we were to be gone, how long we were dropped off at the carnival; and we were timed, we had to be at home by 9:30 p.m.; and we were warned, we were told to be careful. And it turned out that warning was very, very valid because as we were walking around at carnival, we met some schoolmates, some boys, and we didn't pay too much attention, because that is what we were told. We had our rides and then we knew the time was coming that we had to be home. When we started home, it was just the three girls, just myself and my cousin and my younger sister. As we were walking and going towards Coronation Road, we noticed that there was somebody following us, and instead of discouraging them, my younger sister got panicky and she started to run, and the other girl starting running and left me by myself. So I ended up running too because I didn't want to be by myself with these boys that were following, so I went under the train and went on the other side and tried to intercept them at the end of the five cars that were parked there. As I came around the corner, I heard my sister squealing and then the other one laughing too, and I thought, "Oh, no." I was thinking there was something happening, so I ran and went around the corner and I noticed there was somebody running behind me and I thought, "Oh, no." I went around the corner, and everybody was laughing. The boys had caught up to the girls that were running, and the first thing I thought of: we're going to be in trouble, real bad trouble. The three boys were there and asked to walk us home. My first response was, "No, you can't walk us home." They were quite persistent. They said, "Well, we are not going to take no for an answer. We are just going to walk along with you." We knew them very well. We went to school with them. But to me, this was trouble. I knew I was going to be in trouble at home if they came to the door. So they walked along with us until we got close to the house, and I told them, "I don't want to be in trouble." I am responsible for the two young girls that were with me, and if they would be kind enough to let us go in by ourselves. I knew they would bring us right to the door and I knew I would be in trouble.

Even at the time, I had an inkling of what my mother used to say to me about how we have to be careful. I could hear her, hear her words as we were walking along. I guess all the teachings that were being passed down was always in my head. It was not only my mother's side that was very important. Ben Quyxuletse' was the chief of S'amun'a. Before that, we had great grandfather, who married an Indian woman from Snoqualmie, and she married into Songhees. She had a daughter, Suswiw, and she married into Quamichan, to a grandfather—to one of our grandfathers. So we have relatives in the American side. But they used to talk about Indian relations that are far away. Relatives that were from afar. They used to say there is no boundary for the Native People. There was no Canada, there was no USA, and they used to, the chiefs used to marry their sons to other chiefs' daughters from different places.

Sixteen

So when we used to go hop picking in Yakima, we used to stop at this place, a beautiful place, this was Snoqualmie. Great big trees—very, very huge. There was this house. It was about thirty by thirty, or something like that. It was just a wooden floor; it looked like it was just made of lumber, thick lumber, and the floor was just wooden, very, very clean. One great big room with beds in there, a big heater, a kitchen stove, a kitchen wood stove, and that place was my dad's aunt's house. There was Marie, Matilda and Cyrus, a brother. Oh, that was a son. Cyrus was the son of Matilda, and we used to go and visit them every year and stop over there, and they would go into a circle and talk and talk right until the wee hours of the morning. And we'd be talking, and this lady, Marie and Matilda, oh, they used to wear real long skirts, they were kind of jolly, hefty. They used to cook for us and give us boiled meat and potatoes and vegetables, and then she would bring out the jam. We would love having the jam. Homemade jam, blackberry, raspberry, whatever they had. Even apple pies, and we always got to eat the apple pie afterwards. Then we were sent out to play out in the open. It was just like a beautiful park—no bushes just these beautiful trees. I knew them as grand, granny and uncle, Uncle Cyrus and Granny Marie and Granny Matilda. But I never asked how come they were our grannies. Why. It wasn't until much later, and then I start asking questions, and this was just quite awhile later.

Then my dad explained it was his side of the family that they were related to, that they were related from this person that married across to Songhees. It was just recently that I've tried to, this year, before I tried to get the family tree to connect us with the families, the James family from Tulalip. It is very interesting to find out many things about them. Granny Marie had no children, and I would like to make a correction. I have been calling the other one Matilda. It is not Matilda—it is Madeline. Her son was Cyrus. According to Cyrus, the information I got from him, a few years before he passed away, it was a sister of Madeline and Marie. Marie's mother that married into Songhees, and she had a daughter, Suswiw, who married a Cowichan. She was the one that came from the States side, was a daughter of a chief and married a chief from Songhees. Which makes it on my dad's side there was a descendant of a chief from the American side that married his daughter to Songhees.

There is something that my late Uncle Cyrus James said to me. He was saying that the name "qinum"—in our language that our name is from "qinum" in the Cowichan-area language. Uncle Cyrus had said to me that anyone with this ending part of their name would be related to the James family. So in the past since I started working for Songhees, since April of 1997, I have made a list of names and enquired about these people that have the ending -qinum in their name. Indian suffix of -qinum in their name. Of all the names that I have traced, every family that had that ending suffix in their name, I found there was about thirty names, about thirty names that had that ending -qinum in their name. I have asked them where they got the name from, how they got it and where the name was from. Every one of these people, including my grandfather's brother, who was Xut'iqinum, and that name came from Snoqualmie. That was from the James family. All the names that I have traced, it all goes back towards the American side. I would ask, "Where did your name come from?" and a lot of the response would say, "That was from my grandfather from White Rock," which is just next door to Tulalip, not very far from Tulalip. People in the Saanich, Malahat area, I questioned them about their names that have the -qinum ending, and most of them are, well, from their grandfather, most of them came from White Rock, and there were two that came from across Seattle. So that all leads back to confirm what my uncle had said that these people would be related, linking to the family in some way. Many of the families that I have asked about their name with the -qinum ending, they would say that "we know this was my grandfather over here at White Rock, but the name came from further up, either Tulalip, Snoqualmie or La Conner." And with ours it came from Snoqualmie. So in a way, it just confirmed what my Uncle Cyrus James had said about relations with that suffix ending name.

I was already working by the time I was fifteen. I had been working a few years already. My mother used to work for white people for extra money besides her knitting. She used to do housework. At the age thirteen, she starting taking me along with her to start watching, start learning and I used to just go along with her and watch her, first three or four times, and then after she started asking me to help her. The people she worked for were very nice people. I started out working. She was getting about fifty cents an hour, forty-five cents an hour. And the lady started giving me about twenty-five cents an hour for helping her. So I starting working, earning twenty-five cents an hour at the age of thirteen, and my mother was getting about fifty cents. She used to do laundry, she used to wash the floors, polish the floors, wax and polish, and I worked right along with her. Except by the time I was fifteen, I already knew how to do proper procedures of cleaning up: polishing, waxing, laundry and doing housework. By the time I was fifteen, I had jobs too—taking over my mother's job after the school season. I was working in white people's homes to earn money, and from twenty-five cents, I was earning thirty-five cents an hour. That was in 1948. I enjoyed working and earning money. Not very often that I spent it myself. I always spent something for myself and gave the rest to my mother to help out. Because I knew there were other brothers and sisters that needed things.

My brother was a soccer player. He started using my mother's car. But then my mother wanted me to go along with him to make sure that he got home, that he brought the car home. It was all boys, it was stressed to my brother that he had to look after me. So I was with these soccer players. If he took the car, he had to take me along and I had to make sure he came home with the car. There was four, five, six boys on the car and they would go to Victoria, go to Nanaimo—different place to play soccer. One time, it happened that my brother decided he didn't want me to go along. So he said, "OK, we will take her along." Just about a half a mile away, then he says, "OK, you get off, you go home." I said, "No, I can't. Mom said I have to go along." I knew that I was going to be in trouble. They said, "Well, you have to get off." So I ended up getting off and walking home. Well, my brother didn't get the car again. He was in trouble for my getting off the car, and I got into trouble and he got into trouble.

Then I started working at St. Ann's School. I was fifteen and I took another job working in the kitchen and assisting the cook. During the summer months I went back to working for the people I was working for before. Principal of the high school and other places. Farmers. That was when we didn't go across to the States to do strawberries. Most of the time that we went across the States to pick berries, the one that stood out in my mind was the time that we picked berries for a, I think it was a Mr. White, at Mount Vernon. We were picking and making $100 a day. We would get up early in the morning, at the break of dawn, day breaking, and we would be going to the field. It was like that every day, just be getting out of bed and then go up to where the berry fields were. By the time we got there, it would be a bit brighter, so we could see. But that was a challenge.

My parents had decided that they wanted something and that we were all going to work together to get it. It was my mom, dad, my brother Leo and myself and Theresa. One foster sister had to stay home and look after the youngest sister. In one day, it was one dollar a crate: we picked ninety crates—ninety dollars. So for the next day our parents decided we were going to make a hundred dollars and see how long we could hold that. We did that making the hundred dollars a day for about eight days. Eight days, and it was definitely hard work. We worked in the morning without breakfast until 8:30, 9:00 a.m., then we would stop and have something to eat. Something hot would be brought up for us to have. Hot tea, sandwiches. And then we would work again until lunch time, and then there would be a hot pot of soup ready for us to have. Other times we stayed in the fields to save time. We had sandwiches right there in the field. Also, juice would be made and brought up to us.

We were filling all the twenty flats fast, the way we were picking, and I would look back now and then to see what was happening when my dad delivered. He never walked to deliver berries, he ran. And because my brother was a fast picker, he just stayed there and picked, and dad delivered. He'd pack four crates; there was twelve cups to one flat, and he'd pack four flats at a time and then, when he knew he had to do things faster, he would call out and say, "Come and pack one more flat on top," and he'd pack five flats, which is quite heavy.

But we made what we were trying to make. We made our $100 a day. It wasn't only my parents; it was us children that had to work hard. In that one season, we made in four weeks, we made about $2,000 clear. The rest we had spent about $600, $800 towards the food, but that was saved towards the purchase of a tractor. So it was like a lesson to us to showing us what we can do in life. How to do it. We continued into picking raspberries and we cleared a $1,000 in raspberries, which was only about two weeks, and then to cherry picking. That was another $1,000 that we cleared. For the whole season we cleared about $4,000, picking.

We went blackberry picking, and for that the money we made there was spent on our clothes for school. They purchased clothes for when we got home. By the time we came home for school, it was the end of September, October by the time we got home from the season's picking. Other times we went hop picking. Those were after the blackberries—we went hop picking.

There was one time, it was the same. We weren't making as much, but we were making money. There was this one time, they called it Roy's Town. We had left early in the morning; sometimes we used to bring our car out into the field and use the lights to pick until eight, nine o'clock, ten o'clock at night. Go home, go to bed and come out at five o'clock, six o'clock in the morning. One time that we were still picking, and somebody screamed that there was a fire in the camp. Everyone started running. By the time we got to the camp, there were some cabins that were burned down. My dad was running ahead, and my mom was running behind. I wasn't too far behind them. We saw two people that were on top of each other and they were swinging. My dad was going to touch, and my mom knew for some reason that my dad shouldn't touch these people that were swinging around. They were on electric. "You are going to burn," that's all she said. She said, "Get away from there and the people." The people, the ones that were lying on top of the wire were both dead. They were already dead. Two young people. There were in their early twenties. One was twenty-one; the other was twenty-three or twenty-two. Oh, that was really sad. My dad was just ready to grab and pull him off, and my mom screamed. There were wires swinging around. And there were children that were screaming. He detoured himself and went running around and got some of the children out of the cabins. Two cabins were burned down, and it was already going to the next cabin by the time we got there. I can't remember what happened or how that happened. They used to have coal-oil stove, and I think something burned. But the two young people that were going to save, to save their furniture, and they ended up dying instead. So there were some tragedies in our travels earning money. But things do happen. The young lady was a Harry, the mother was American. She was from Augie Harry's daughter, I think. I can't really remember. I think her name was Agnes. That was sad, sad times. This was in Tacoma. Other times we travelled all the way to Yakima. That was way before that burning in Tacoma camp.

Seventeen

THERE WAS EARLIER TIMES. There was something that I wondered how, why my mother let me. I was working at St. Ann's, St Ann's School as an assistant cook and earning money, and I wasn't earning very much. I was only getting seventy-five dollars a month. If I worked extra, it wasn't very much. She used to allow me to take money out. My brother used to ask our auntie, Mrs. Robbie Daniels, to have a dance. It would just be family and a few friends, but my aunt and uncle at Cowichan Bay, used to open their house and let us have a dance. My brother was sixteen, I was fifteen. With the ten dollars I'd buy bologna, four loaves of bread (they were large loaves of bread), lettuce, butter, mayonnaise, for sandwiches and pop. Two dozen pop. We would invite other teenagers that were the same age, thirteen-, fourteen-, fifteen- and sixteen-year-olds. And my aunt, who was Mrs. Robbie Daniels, who was older than my dad, she would say, "Well, you can use my living room and your uncle and I will be here. You make your sandwiches. You stay here until ten, eleven o'clock, and that's fine with us." So we would make our sandwiches and we never stayed later than 10:30. Even though they said eleven o'clock. It was my parents that said we had to be home earlier.

This was just about twice a month that we did that, and one time, older boys got there. Young men that were in their twenties, and my aunt's husband, Robbie Daniels, he got up and he went out. They pushed their way in. They were going to join us, they wanted to, they said they wanted to be with us. But they were drinking, so my uncle came out and told them they weren't welcome. That it was only invited people that could come to his place and that these young men were not welcome to come. He knew all of them, he knew who they were, where they were from, but he didn't appreciate their drinking. So they couldn't stay. They were upset, they were mad, but Uncle was very firm and said, "No, we don't want you."

It was a very friendly time—we always had a nice time, we always enjoyed ourselves. We all danced, rock and roll. My brother had all the records, and we all enjoyed being together with these relatives and cousins, so we thought that was alright. And I really think that my parents and family had something to do with this. This was to keep the soccer team, which my brother was in, from drinking and to help them out from doing other things, doing something else besides drinking, and being chaperoned by my aunt and uncle. This went on for about two years. Maybe even more. I guess it kind of made me wonder—I was allowed to spend my money on the goodies for the teenagers. I guess our Elders were very smart. They knew how to have us look after each other. My brother had the responsibility of looking after me, and I had the responsibility of looking after him. And then having chaperones.

No matter what time of the year, there was always responsibilities of having to do something before we had our dance party. Or, if there was something going on in the community that one always came first. The chores, the responsibility, and then we were allowed to do, allowed to go to soccer or have a dance or just a show. I was allowed to go to the dances but I was not allowed to get involved with anyone. The people that were at these teen dances, most of them were related. Soccer players weren't relatives; they were distant relatives. But to me they were just close friends. There was no involvement, and we just enjoyed dancing with one another and talking.

We were allowed to go to a few of the other parties that were going on. This was at the old armoury. My brother and myself, we went to this dance, and we were warned to be careful of who we talked to, who we were friendly with, and I thought that that was. I guess I really didn't understand what she meant by that. After a while I realized my brother was getting involved with someone, that he was interested in a girl. Then young men that were much older than me were talking to me, and I had told my mother. Her response was this: I was told, "This is what I told you was going to happen." She told me she had predicted this was going to happen. She said, "Well, you can't get involved with that person. They are from a different background." I didn't understand what that meant. When she said "different background," I thought she meant that as an Indian . . . I guess I just didn't understand what she meant. To me, I thought it was because the person I was talking about was from another reserve, and that was different. I had no inkling that she was taking about our background of ourselves as Indian people. I thought all Indians were the same, were equal.

By this time, she had already started telling me I had to, she started reminding me back of the times I had heard the Old People talking and reminding me of who I was and what I am going to be. I thought, well, aren't all people like that? That is when she really started opening up and telling me that all Native People weren't like that. Meaning like that, being a Thi'tha, holding the Rattler and Mask and being able to bless a house, bless water, cleanse people. There are many things that we do. I guess the explanation was there were other people that were, or that held people in things, but not as much as we had. She started naming these people from other areas, like Kuper Island, Chemainus Bay, Nanaimo, Song-hees, Saanich, North Vancouver and Musqueam. Naming people from all the areas, different areas, Westholme. Then what really woke me up was when we were going with her to different places. But to me, going with her was part of the life that as a Native person I thought all Indians did the same thing. I thought that everybody did the things that we did. It was about the time I was fifteen that I really realized that there was something different, that I was already into something that I was trained for. That she had trained me, and I didn't really realize that I was already trained to be something, to belong to something, to know how to take care of things, and I thought everyone was the same. I guess that really woke me up, that, waking up to the fact that not everybody was the same, and that someday that getting married was coming, was going to happen. The warnings about being careful, watch yourself, who you go with. It never really made sense until much later, what she meant.

Then my brother getting married and having a child. The things that my brother, in a way refusing, and yet not really refusing, but not really participating in the things that he was supposed to be participating in. He was very well aware of things that we were trained for. He followed to an extent, but, in a way, he didn't want to participate. I still don't understand why he didn't participate. But when that happened, it fell on me that I had to be the one, and by this time, my mother started changing her words—that things, that everything was going to be up to me. OK, you are going to have to start thinking this, that everything that you are getting, you are going to be responsible not only for yourself, your future, when that someday you will have children, you will be responsible for that.

The words changed from my brother, everything going to my brother first, everything gradually changed and came towards me; and OK, you are going to do this, you are going to be the one. Your brother, if he has children, then you are going to be responsible. I just took it in without saying yes or no because what was said to me was—it felt like it was already made up, already decided. It wasn't like I was going to have to decide whether I accept or don't accept. It was decided by my parents, grandparents, the Elders, just about everyone seemed to have decided something that I couldn't say that I, that I couldn't do. When it was decided, it was decided that I do it; and you can't say no and you can't even ask a question. You just accept, and that is what I was told. You can't question an Elder and say, "What am I going to be doing?" You can't decide for yourself. You can't say that you can't do it, because you are going to do it. So I just accepted whatever was decided, from the Elders. It was not only my mother. It was my uncles and aunts, my grandparents.

Later on, at sixteen, I met the children's father. Ronald George was logging with my dad for Evans Lumber Company. I went to a show, and he walked me home and then left me at the door and he left. Then after we went to carnival, he brought me home again. Twice, and the Old People started saying you are seeing somebody. I just saw him twice and then I went to show again. He came and took me to show and back home, and then that was getting serious. And I said, "Well, I have seen him only three times." They said, "We know the young man. We know who he is, we know where he comes from. You can't just fool around." And I thought, "Oh, my God, gee." I tried to say I wasn't fooling around, but it was already there, decided. My parents had already decided that I wasn't going to be just seeing this young man that is coming to see me. From the fourth time he came, they confronted him and asked him what his intentions were. He said he wanted to keep seeing me. He wanted to take me out again. And they told him outright if you have serious intentions, then you have to decide. Either you let her go or you decide to get married. We were both just fifteen. I was working at St. Ann's. I went back to school for one year and finished grade eight. After, I worked again at St. Ann's, and then this must have been in August, because by November 27, we were both sixteen, we got married.

When he said that he was going to marry me, then Dad gave him a job, and he went logging with my dad and my brother. Sixteen years old, and he was logging. But then, my brother started logging at fifteen, and I was working at St. Ann's still. By November 27, we were married. September before that, we were announced and we saw the priest, and I was very well known to the Sisters of St. Ann's. It turned out to be a big wedding. It wasn't only my parents' involvement; it was the Sisters of St. Ann's because I was working there. The sisters got involved too. They became the choir for the mass at the wedding and they were all excited, and then my dad gave me a little house. We had a little tiny house. This was something that the priest suggested, that we should live in our own place, so my dad gave me a house, land and house. Father LeClair helped drywall the place and fixed it up,

St. Ann's School, Duncan, BC. St. Ann's School was established in 1864 for Indigenous girls. In 1904 it became St. Ann's Boys School. From 1956 to 1964 it was a day school for both boys and girls. The school closed in 1964, but continued as a residence for sisters. In 1979, the property was leased to the Vancouver Island Providence Community (Memory BC).
Jay Powley, 1945.

furnished it, and they had Ronald, my dad, Father LeClair worked every evening to make the house look really nice. We had the Sisters of St. Ann's for the choir. So, we had our wedding. Turned out, his family from Saanich came, Walter Williams and his family, they all came to the wedding, and Sisters of St. Ann's were involved. We had dinner reception at Koksilah at the old Big House. That is where the reception was. The reception was held at a Longhouse, but the kitchen part had no flooring, just dirt floor. Long tables. But we were all happy.

Ruby and Ronald's wedding, in 1948.
Courtesy of Molly Peter. Photographer unknown, 1948.

And I stayed on my job at St. Ann's. I worked at there for a
long time. And then I had, during the summer, there was no work
there, because the boys were gone, so I would work around the
area with the other jobs I had. Housekeeping jobs, private homes
that I knew where I was always hired. I never had any children the
first year and then I still followed my mother, still followed her
wherever she went.

Eighteen

B Y THIS TIME, IT WAS 1950. I was getting a dollar an
hour. I had quite a few places to go to. Different places. 1951, I
still had no baby, and my mother was starting to worry. By summertime she was asking, asking and worrying and telling me how
hard it is to be without children. Then she started saying, "Well,
I want to have grandchildren before I get too old. I want to see
grandchildren. I want a lot of grandchildren." Then she started
telling me, "Maybe you are like me, like the way I was. You aren't
going to have any children unless you do something about it."
This was summertime already. Summertime in 1951.

Then I finally agreed with her. I guess I always wanted to please
my mother. I guess in a way I understood what she saying. So she
decided she was going to give me what was given to her by her
aunt. And she brought me to this old lady that gave her those
herbs to have children, so I met her. I can't remember her name.
But we went for the herbs ourselves. Tromping in the forest, and
she said, "I know where it is. Follow me." So I was following her
around. "This is the one." So we started picking some. She said, "I
don't remember which one is for the boy, to have a boy." She asked
me if it mattered, and I said to me a baby was a baby and I was
willing to try. So this was in October and she says, "OK, we'll just
follow the directions of how to use it and when to use it. At what
my aunt, how she taught me. You'll take it just the same way." So
I did exactly as she told me. She made it for me to drink. She said,

"A certain day you are going to have to drink this." So that certain day came, and then she said, "Well, you take it, drink it, that's it—you just forget about it. Don't think about it. We'll just wait."

And that was it. That was what she told me. So I drank it and then just put it out of mind and not even think about it. But it worked. Right to the day, July 3, and my baby was born. I got pregnant and I had my baby nine months later. I was still farming for my dad at six months of being pregnant. The sisters and Father LeClair were worried and stressed.

I didn't go to a doctor, why I wasn't conceiving. She, my mother, just decided I was like her. She was just so happy, so thrilled that it worked. That she was going to have a grandchild. It didn't matter to her if it was a girl or a boy, and it didn't matter to me whether it was a boy or a girl, but just that it was going to be a baby. That was all—we just wanted a baby. She was so happy when my baby was born, and she said, "Well, you've got a girl. You remember the herb you took had a flower, and that's for a girl." It wasn't a mistake; it was just that was how it went. We weren't trying to choose if it was a boy or a girl—we just did it. She was so happy. She said that I was getting blessed with a girl. That a girl was the most important, that this girl, this first born is going to be the mother hen of the future children that I was going to have. She was going to be the mother hen of them because she was the oldest, and it was true, it was so true. My daughter, she was a delicate little thing, delicate. Yet she was strong.

By the time she was three. I didn't get pregnant again until 1953, didn't have my second baby until '54. The funny thing is that, in a way, my mom was happy, yet she was cautious. And then she says, "OK, to space your children, make sure you nurse your baby." Not only her, it was the other Elders that were concerned about how I was going to feed this baby, whether I was going to be nursing this baby or not. There was this old lady that was by Buckerfield's that was my husband's grandmother. I brought my baby to her, her great-granddaughter, and that was the first question she asked: "How are you feeding your baby? Are you giving her cow's milk or are you breastfeeding her?" She started praising the Lord that I wasn't feeding my baby animal milk, as she said in Indian. She started clapping her hands, thanking God that I was not feeding her great-granddaughter animal milk, which meant cow's milk, or any kind of animal, I guess. Or they used to use what? Goat's milk too? This made the Elders happy, that I was breastfeeding. It was important to the older people and to my mother—it was part of spacing my child from getting pregnant. So my second baby didn't come until 1954, '52, '54, and then we were very happy in those days. My husband was working steady, logging. My children, they were growing up healthy. They were happy children.

My mother had cattle, which we were helping her look after. It seemed like she always had cattle; her father had cattle, and that's how she always got by—having cattle. When she needed money, she always sold cattle to make ends meet or to get equipment. When were at our own place, we were always looking after her cattle, which were in our field. Helping her, helping Dad with looking after them. Even though we were married, we still had worked together with my parents. Kept busy with the farm.

I guess I never really realized that I was really attached to my parents, even though I was married, even though I was now in a different home. My parents were always there, or I was always at their place. We were always doing things together, working things together, helping each other. There was never-ending work to helping one another.

Then when I had my second son, I kept my job as a housekeeper. It was just not quite a year later. I got pregnant very early with my second son. And then my first, my second child, the third child—another boy—were only fifteen months apart. They were very close together. We lived in the little house for many years. I used to have visitors from Sisters of St. Ann, the priests, they used to walk down to my place. Walk down and say their prayers. I was always expecting them. My mother always taught me that. That when you wake up, the first thing you do is straighten yourself up because you are going to have visitors. Never stay in bed. Never think you aren't going to have visitors. The first thing to do is clean up, straighten up the house. What she taught was so very true. When my husband went to work early in the morning, and

I happened to be staying home, that is the first thing I did. Clean up and be ready for visitors.

I always had visitors: priests, sisters, Elders and, of course, my mother was there quite often. Some just stayed for a cup of coffee and discussion and gone again. We had visitors, many Elders coming to see, to be with the children. And I had an uncle, he was hard of hearing. He always came by to see if I needed help, to check up on me. He used to often take my children for a walk, short walks. He would come in early, and I would give him coffee, toast and something to eat, then he would grab the children and say, "I am taking the children for a walk." He would take them off my hands for a few hours. If I wasn't keeping up the house, then I was working somewhere else, doing housework to earn extra money to help financially. That was stressed to me, that we save a little nest egg for something, and we bought a car—we bought a used car.

When my first son was born, we bought a used car, and my husband had joined the Junior Native Sons Soccer. So weekends, he used to go play a tournament. Sometimes I went along, sometimes I didn't. He practised twice a week. I used to enjoy watching those games, but my Elders used to tell me, "You remember that there is hard times in marriages, in all marriages, that there is going to be ups and downs in your marriage." I had sensed that he had started drinking with his soccer buddies, and this was the warning that the Elders were talking about, the ups and downs that was going to come.

It was hard when that started happening. The times that I ended wondering if he was going to make it home. Sometimes he was riding with somebody and going to Victoria and not coming home. But then I had the car. I was just worried about him not making it home. But it was when he was driving that made me worry quite a bit. My mother used to pick me up and say, "Well, let's get, I will drive you, and we'll get the car home if he doesn't come home." But he always came home, so that was when I found him, just about knew where to find him.

That went on for a while. Then he just started listening to the Elders that were lecturing him and telling him that was he was doing was very wrong and that things aren't going to get any better. He was risking losing his family. Who is more important? Your friends or your wife and children? Then he decided he was going to quit drinking altogether. He didn't drink anymore for more than ten years. We more or less just concentrated on the children, and my mother got me more involved with the teachings, and then I guess the Elders had been talking together. I know they were, I knew they were talking, but I didn't, I never paid attention to what they were discussing every time they were together. I was always around them. They always either came to my house, my parents' place, and the next thing I knew, they approached me about becoming a band councillor. They had decided that I had all the teachings to know, to understand. The education. So it seemed that they concentrated on what I was going to do. How they were going to go about it—me becoming a councillor. It was not only me. It was my cousin, Xut'iqinum, Dennis Alphonse. They had decided they were going to get us involved with more than just committees. It wasn't only the Elders; it was the whole community. Any function that was going on, whether it was gathering for winter dance, memorial, funerals, anything that was going on, I had to be there among the people and helping out financially to anyone that was having something to do with the Longhouse or memorial. The way was to get involved in something, was to be among the people. To get to know the people as well as the different kinds of functions that were going on in the community. So it seemed like I was pushed into doing more than just my home activity.

But outside my home activity, there's other things that I had to attend to, as well as the training that I was getting from my mother about the things that were going to be passed on to me and the children. One thing that was said: I was often told, "The teachings that we are giving you isn't the same as other communities. There are other communities, other families that have different teaching." To me, when that was said to me, what was different about the teachings that I was being given, from other families? I couldn't grasp what that meant. Why was my teaching different? How was it different? My teaching from other families. I thought, they are Indians, they are hwulmuhw. How come they should be different? I never understood what that meant for many years, so every time that question came into my head, I always thought, "Well, I guess I will realize someday; maybe there is something that I am not supposed to ask. I am not supposed to ask what it is."

So the Elders just sort of gave me all the things that they thought was important for them to pass on to me. They were filling me with all the teachings that belonged to them, two different families, but they were all related. So all the ones that are related, their teachings are quite similar. I didn't know the meaning of the different teaching until way later, until after my mom was gone, and then I start thinking, "What is this different teaching?" The teaching that my extended family kept talking about and wondering why there was different teachings. Thinking back on what was being said to me over and over, then repeating it to my own children later on, I guess it just sort of made me realize that I was just so protected by my own extended family. I was being filled up with all these teachings, and I thought that was the same all over, that all Natives had the same teachings. But that is not so. There is a different teaching at different Longhouses.

Nineteen

We USED TO GO TO DIFFERENT LONGHOUSES. I used to go with my mother. Then thinking back on all the things that she said, all the lectures that she made in different Longhouses when she gave somebody teachings, I realized later, that what she was telling them was for that Longhouse. If she was at Clem Clem, she gave them the teachings, that she knew all the teachings in that Longhouse, so the teaching she gave them was teachings that belonged to that Longhouse. If she was at Somenos, she knew the teachings there, so she gave them that teachings. Because there was three different Longhouses on different reserves. And she was always called to preach to young people. Whether it was a new dancer, or an orphan, or coming into maturity. She was called on to tell them how they should be when, how they have to look after themselves when they become orphaned; or if they are a dancer, what they have to follow. Because I listened to so much teachings that, to me, I just put it into one, and thinking that it was just one teachings. It was not. These were all separate for different areas— she knew the teachings to each area, so she brought it out to how they understood it and how they handled it.

It took me a long time to realize this. To separate all the things that she was talking about, all the things that she had said and listening to the Elders that were around me and thinking about it. Separating all the different areas and all the family teachings for different things—for the Mask Dance, for the Rattlers, for death, for marriage—and I had to separate all this and figure them out, and then I heard myself saying the same thing to my own children as to what I heard from my Elders. It's almost word for word what was said to me and what I have been saying to my children. I am trying to be a little bit more careful to try and make them really understand what I am saying now.

Even when I was having my children and how they, my Elders, sat me down and how they talked to me, right from when I became pregnant, my role as the dos and don'ts of pregnancy, what you don't eat, like the rock cod. What happens when you eat rock cod, what does it do? I was just told that it causes seizures. And liver, when you eat liver, whether it's the deer liver or the cow liver, that it causes murmurs in the heart; and the back bone of the deer, the ribs or the bottom rump of the backbone causes that baby to be a crybaby. The ribs, deer ribs—why don't we eat it? When you are expecting, you are not supposed to eat the ribs because it can cause a protrusion in the baby's ribs. Strawberries: there is a way that you can eat strawberries without getting strawberry on your baby when you are expecting. You have to scare the strawberry, and there are words that you can use. And that's exactly what I did.

And the waterfowl, if you eat both legs of the waterfowl, then the baby's hips will be close together, just the way the waterfowl is, and walk just like that. Fish heads and the tail: if you eat the tail part of the fish, then your baby will be breach. And the heads: I used to laugh when they used to tell me that if you eat the heads that the baby's head will be moving—there's a name for it, but I don't know the English part—but just like your head will be moving all the time, that the baby's head will be shaking all the time. Crabs: if you are eating crabs and if you don't drink water, then your baby will walk like a crab, and I found this to be true. I have grandchildren, my daughter was eating crabs, and they are crawling sideways. When you eat a smul'sh—crab—real soft. We know of one lady that ate that, the one that was really soft—it turned out her baby had no bones on her ankle. It was just jelly. She put her baby away, and that baby should be thirty-two now. When it walked, it just rolled around. Peanuts, oysters, clams: if you eat those, then your womb will be hard to break for you to have your baby. They say we should never cut fish, and it was only the dog salmon that we were told not to cut when we were expecting, and I found this to be true because one of my own had a cleft palate. And I always felt responsible because I brought the fish over, and the young lady cut the fish and cut the palate of her baby, and one of my grandchildren was born with a cleft palate. There's a lot of things that they even used to tell us: not play with animals or snakes, play with snakes or anything that looks awful. If we saw anything dirty, you are supposed to spit and not swallow. I followed all of these when I was expecting.

And the father, when the baby is born, they have to go for a bath, get up early, do a lot of things, work: just like waking their being up when they have their first child. I found this to be true because my brother-in-law, when he married my sister, he was as slow like a snail, and when he had his first child, he was told to get up early and sleep on the floor. He slept on the hard floor and he went for a bath early in the morning. He packed wood and ran, did things really fast. He broke out of his laziness, and even when he was working out in the woods, he worked really fast without injuring himself. He always worked in a fast pace. And anywhere where he worked in logging, setting, choking, he got himself a name, to the point that if he finished one job, he was hired at another place because he had a good name for the kind of work he did. Even the new mother has to do things to wake her spirit so she won't be just sleeping while her baby is crying. Not to be lazy. What you have to do: blow your eyes[1] to wake yourself in the morning, the first four mornings.

There's many things we were told we had to follow. Like the changing of a young man. The kw'unt'als, I forgot the English name of that rock [basalt] that had to be used on the man so he won't have big breasts, like a woman's breasts. That's what was used to rub on his chest so he wouldn't have woman's breasts. Children in the cemetery—they never used to let children go in the cemetery

---

1 This is done ritually to wake the spirit when a person undergoes life changes such as puberty, being orphaned, initiation into the Longhouse or giving birth.

because their souls aren't, they aren't strong enough to fight off the spirits in cemeteries. These are only some of the teachings that we were given. That was for the pregnancy, for a young couple and their child when they are coming of age. And different places they handle the changing of a child to an adult, puberty, for a boy and a girl. It was handled different many years ago. They have different teachings in different areas. What they do to young people is the same with the Longhouse. They have different teachings too, as to how they handle their dancers. New dancers, what they have to do in training. And with orphans, what has to be done about the orphans. That is the first four days after the funeral. All in the Cowichan area, they are all similar to one another—Quamichan, Somenos, Clem Clem—their teachings are very close together, but in other areas there might be a slight difference.

With the orphans, before the funeral, they can't touch forks or anything that is sharp. Knives, needles, safety pins, broom, rakes, axe—they can't use these. They have to call a Thi'tha, someone that knows how to work, knows how to sing the song or the prayers for all these things. There is only Esther and myself that do that around here, and her son and my children that can do these things. And there is a reason for not being able to use any sharp things. When I asked what was the purpose of this, all these sharp things that has to be worked on, the Elders said it was a preventative. To prevent the families from hurting one another. That was for their future, so they won't hurt each other. Hurting someone or even hurting themselves. I did find this to be true just recently.

A young man came to me. He was orphaned about five years, and because I'm an Elder, he didn't know where to go, so he thought of me, so he came to ask me, "What can I do to, what's causing me to hurt myself all the time? What did I do? What happened? I am a carver, and every time I work with my knife, I cut myself. I worked with an axe and I accidentally chopped myself. I worked with a saw and I got cut on the hip with the saw, a power saw." And he was naming different things that were happening to him. And then after he was telling me, I asked him, "Well, you became a dancer. Did they do something for you?" He said, "Yes, they did." I said, "When you became an orphan, did they do anything for you?" He said he didn't remember. So I told him to come back the next morning and I will get things ready.

He got there early the next morning, and I had everything ready, the tumulh ochre paint and some grease, some water and towels. I had my cedar stick and board to drum on. I had the needle, scissor, knife, axe, paddle. I said, "OK, we'll see how you are after this." So I did what had to be done. I worked on him, and he left. It was about six months later, and I saw him, and he says, "Oh, hi, Auntie. I'm all cured." I said, "You're OK?" He says, "I'm fine. I haven't had any accidents. I haven't cut myself. I do fine with a power saw. I am all right." I said, "OK, that is where it was. You didn't get worked on after you became an orphan. That's how important it is that you follow the rules." And he said he couldn't remember whether it was done or not. I said if you couldn't remember then maybe it wasn't done. So that proved a point for him and it showed that things can happen, because he was a dancer and he had followed the rules before, but he didn't after he lost his parents.

It seemed like from my childhood to my adulthood, to my marriage, it seemed like I was following rules and rules and rules and rules. Having Elders around me all the time, and it got to the point that, I guess, being used to listening to the Elders talk about rules, that I always kind of waited for somebody to tell me all these things, all the rules about this and rules about that. Even the rules about how to raise your child. How you are going to treat them, from the time the mother is expecting and talking to the baby when they are still in the mother's tummy. I did this with my youngest daughter and her baby on her last eight months and ninth months and her baby was very active in her tummy. I used to speak Indian, speak Indian to her baby, telling him that he was going to be a soccer player and he didn't have to be kicking around now, he can wait, and talking gently to the baby she was carrying. And now I find that after baby was born, and every time he fusses, if he started fussing I start speaking Indian to him. He would sit there and listen to me and stop fussing or getting angry or whatever. Then he would start listening to me when I speak Indian to him. And that is exactly what I used to do to him when he was in his mom's tummy, and he used to stop and not kick around, because he was so active in her tummy that she used to get so worn out and tired. I find that whenever her little son is angry, as soon as I start speaking Indian to him, he stops and listens to me.

This is something that the Old People used to talk about. They used to talk about talking to the baby when they are still in the mother's tummy and that they can hear you. I always thought, "Is it possible? Is it true?" They used to say you could talk to them and tell them things. And that is exactly what my daughter used to do. She used to talk to her baby, and I did the same thing to her too; and after baby was born, he always paid attention when I spoke our language, and I often talk to him in our language, and he'd look at me and then he'd listen. He always stopped fussing and listened to me. That is exactly what the Old People used to say. You start early; they used to tell me that you think a child does not understand, but as long as a child can hear, they can understand. Maybe they can't voice speak, but they can understand; and the parents, they used to say, it's the parents that raise the child the way they are, that they become. If you raise your child for something, to do something, then that's how they will be. You have to listen and teach them things.

And then as I was having children, my mother used to say the same thing to me. "Remember your child is a human being, your child is somebody." The way you talk to your child is the way they are going to be when they grow up—how you talk to your children, how you discipline them. Remember, don't ever spoil them, giving in to them at everything they want. Sure, they are cute, cuddly, they're beautiful when they are small, but if you spoil that child, you will have no control. You won't be able to tell them anything. They won't listen to you. So you start teaching a child at a very, very early age. By listening, the tenderness in your voice, how you say no, whether you mean it or you don't mean it. They know every sound, every look you give them. They know you. How you look at them, how you give them love, how you feed them.

Twenty

A s MY CHILDREN WERE GROWING, by the time I had my third one, and that is when my uncle came in—well, he was always there, but he became more close. He was deaf, he couldn't hear. You really had to holler to make him hear. And this was something. My children never noticed that there was something wrong with him. He played with them just normally—with the way we talk—and it's really surprising how a child can communicate with somebody that is hard of hearing. My children got attached to my uncle, my oldest, my second and my third. They used to play outside. We had a German shepherd, Chinook, that was very well trained. We always had animals: cats, dogs, chickens and cattle. My uncle would come and help me by taking my children off my hands and taking them for walks. It never occurred to me, I never thought about it, that he was hard of hearing, that there was a problem. I didn't think of it as a problem. I was just happy when he was there. I was able to communicate sometimes with my hands and sometimes I talk really loud at him, and he'd answer me back. I guess I was told that you don't, at an early age, you don't make fun of people that have problems. You don't criticize, you don't laugh at them, you treat them equal to you. And that is exactly what I did with all the ones that were around me, that were always around me. That's how I treated them, how I cared for the Elders. I used to do a lot of canning because that is what I learned when I was working at St. Ann's. All different fruits and fish and meat, venison. It was all canned.

One time my uncle went out, and I thought, "How did he communicate with my kids?" I guess I did get curious one time. There was a bush that came from the road and going down into the field. I used to walk down and feed the cattle. I was coming back, and they were walking along the road, and I started listening, and they were answering each other, and I thought, "My God, that communication was right open." It was really, really something to hear, a four-year-old boy and a man who is hard of hearing, and they were communicating, by just talking normal—answering each other. I kind of laughed to myself because I thought that was kind of funny and interesting.

All the Old People used to be around us. Just about this time of year, spring time, that my uncle, Manson George. I used to drive all the Old People to Victoria. My mother would say, "You are going to drive us to Victoria this weekend." I would never know who is "we." Sometimes it was Mr. and Mrs. Antoine and my parents, or Mr. and Mrs. Johnnie George and my grandparents, or Mr., Mrs. Antoine, Isaac Antoine, and drive them to Victoria and back. They would go shopping. Shop in Victoria. Shop for clothes, some new things and some used clothing and some furniture. Whatever they needed. I was told I couldn't say no, I always had to—if they needed me, I had to go. Sometimes I was by myself that would do the driving because my dad and the children's father were logging and they would have gone to work, and then I'd drive the other Elders to do some shopping.

It was decided that they were going to build a barn, a barn for the cattle. I heard them talking and I thought they were just kind of laughing and talking: "Well, I'll be the foreman, and you be the second foreman, and we'll get the poles and then lumber—oh, we know where there is some lumber." They would ask me if I had some money and they knew, I guess my mother was probably telling them, that I had savings. So they decided that they were going to build a barn and spent my money. I didn't question them, I didn't object, I just said, "OK," that was fine with me. That was what had to be done, and my mother said that these are Elders, and that'll be a souvenir, and they will be long gone and the barn will still be here. So the work went on: poles and timber were all brought in from our own field, from the forest part of the sixteen acres. They were all cut and peeled. It was just made, cut right from the forest except for the lumber. Young people that did the hard work were the children's father, and my uncle Frances George and Arvid Charlie. They all pitched in, and my dad was still quite strong then, so he helped a lot. They all worked together with the older ones, my grandfather, Alphonse George and Manson George as the foreman, second foreman. It seemed like every day there was to be a big meal at the end of the day and a lot of discussion afterwards at the table, and sometimes we had our supper at my mother's place, which was a bigger place to go to because my house was quite small.

It was at this time that someone was murdered. We were already quite aware of the residential school problems by then. The alcohol that was going on. The different problems arising from the time we were in school and from the time that residential school children were grown up already. This murder that happened was on Kuper Island. At that time, the man came to us was a relative of the one that was attached to my dad, William Paul. He came and he asked my mother to borrow some money to save his grandson from a death sentence. My mother told him she had used her funds, but she told him, "My daughter has a nest egg. You might be able to get it from my daughter." I didn't know how to react. It kind of upset me that I was pointed out to help out, but I couldn't say anything. I couldn't say no, because he was an Elder, so I helped him. I got the money that he asked for from the credit union and I gave it to him. He was in tears of gratitude that I was helping him. This was a time that his cousin was supposed to come home and sign over some land to me. That was the help he was getting from him. They were going to sign a piece of land to me.

Well, I guess that money did help a little because instead of the gallows, he was sentenced and he was out eventually. He got out. But that seemed to be only the beginning of the problems that we were facing now. All the problems that came from the punishment we got and losing the teachings that were being handed down to us. I was just lucky that I wasn't in residential school, that I was surrounded by Elders giving me teachings and telling what to do, helping me out in every way that they could. And it was all for the future, and that barn was part of it. The joy that was about that barn being built; the happiness that went with it was really something to see. We had pictures of them building the barn—I don't know where that is now. It was just happiness and accomplishment that would stay with us for years and years. From 1955, that barn was built, and that was about forty-three years ago, and it is still there. The teachings that was carried with all that, the love that came with it, from the Elders.

They were seeing the children that were there. By the time that I had my fourth child, my son, and then there was a death in Comiaken. Because they had no place to place them, they were placed with me. A little boy, only six months old, and a girl, two-year-old. So I became a foster parent. I had five children. My house was getting too small. We asked for an addition, which they gave us eventually. It was the same with these children, whether they are yours or not, the love that they should receive from you, the tenderness, the caring: treat them as your own. Those were all the words that I received from the Elders. Then my mother always said, "Study your children; don't forget to study your children. Every child is different. Their personality is different from the other. They aren't going to be identical: don't ever, don't ever compare your children to the other, because every child is going to be different from the other. Their likes, their dislikes, study them so you will know them. Each one of them is going to be different. Even your foster children. You will have to get to know them by heart. Their actions, how they are; when they are sad, when they are happy; their likes, their dislikes. But don't ever compare any child to the other and say you should be like your brother, you should be like your sister. Never use those words. Treat them as they are, as you see them."

I followed their advice. "If you are going to be angry at them all the time, that's how they'll be. They will be angry for the rest of their lives. Treat them with tenderness, and that is how they will be. But don't ever spoil them. Don't give them everything they cry for. Especially when it comes to candy. Treat them every now and then, but not to the point that you are spoiling them." This I never understood. How do you spoil your child? Well, I found out. It wasn't my first son that went into a tantrum—it was one of them. And then I learned that you can spoil a child. But I was always told, "Don't forget your Elders, don't forget your Elders, don't forget to respect yourself."

Twenty-one

BY THIS TIME, we were being bred, Dennis Alphonse and myself, to become councillors. That was in 1958? There was a reason. I guess there was always a reason for all the attention that I was getting from the Elders. There was a chief and council election; we had barely even talked about the problems in Cowichan people, even thought about it, but I wasn't made aware of that. I was just gradually being trained, being led into something that I had to do. The work that went with everything, the work that I did. Thinking back about all these things, yes, I guess in a way I sensed it, and maybe I didn't want to admit it but I, maybe I knew what was going on.

I was always looking after the Elders, and then later on my uncle's wife died and grandma died and then Mrs. Antoine died. Those were all sad times. Really hard. Then my uncles all became bachelors. That didn't stop them from visiting me. Their visits became kind of spaced, but they were always there, or I was always around them in the Longhouse.

I would take them to store at least twice a month. Once a month, every time they got their pension. One of them would phone me, and say, "Pick me up." That would be at ten o'clock in the morning. I would pick one up and then go pick the other uncle up. "OK, there is one more uncle you have to pick up." They would talk and laugh. They were all together, my three uncles. There was four, there was Little Joe. By this time, I had another child. I would bring them to town, and by this time when we got to town and got the checks cashed, they'd say, "You must shop for me, and we'll go and wait for you. You have to go and shop." That was really funny. I never got to refuse; I never thought it was wrong or anything like that. All I thought was, "Well, they want me to shop, so I am going to shop." And then they'd say, "Drive this way, drive over there, turn in here," so I would turn. That was the Tzouhalem Hotel. They would say, "Come in, come in!" So I would go in and sit with them, and they would start telling me what they needed, what they wanted me to buy, and I'd write it all down, and they would tell me "OK." Each one of them would give me about sixty dollars each. That's for the whole month's meat. Whatever they decided they needed.

By the time I finished, my trunk was full, and by the time I got finished shopping, that's over two hours of shopping at Overwaitea, then I'd go and pick them up. And oh—they were happy. They were always happy I did all the shopping. I got all what they needed, all labelled who belonged to who, and I would bring them home. Every month that went on, twice a month, the shopping. I never thought—I never said, "I am sorry, I am busy." I was always taught to care for my Elders.

My uncles said not to pay attention to anyone, because I had heard some talk from other people saying I was stealing money from Elders, and when I told them this, they said, "Let them think what they want. It is us that trusts you. We are the ones that chose for you to be doing the things we ask you to do for us. Don't listen to them." I guess it did look bad in other people's eyes and seeing these Old People giving me money and me putting it in my purse. It looked like I was stealing from them. That is what I was accused of: stealing from Old People. So I listened to them, told them, "I'm not going to listen. Just let them talk because that is not what I am doing, I am not stealing." But I didn't think that anything was going to happen, and it was just after I had taken the money and assured them I'll be back later on, and they were just going to sit in the beer parlour and wait for me.

I walked out of the beer parlour, little realizing that someone had followed me. I got out the door and then I heard someone screaming at me. And I looked back and saw this lady and I just ignored her, and that got her more mad. I had long hair—my hair was up to my hips—and I just kept on walking away from her, and next thing I know, she got ahold of my hair. She was screaming, "You thief, stealing from old men!" I said, "They are my uncles." "I saw you, I saw you stealing their money." Tried reasoning with her, and she wouldn't. She had my hair. She locked her hands in my hair. She just kept screaming about my being a thief and all that and swearing at me. I couldn't do anything because of the way she was holding, the way she had locked her hands in my hair. So I turned around, and much as my head was hurting, I turned around and I bumped her in the chest and I threw her against the door. I had pushed her right to the door. She still wouldn't let me go. There was no one around. I was alone; I couldn't get any-body's attention. My uncles didn't realize what was happening, and I don't know how I did it, but I managed to punch her and broke her teeth. As soon as that happened, my hands swelled up with teeth marks on it, and she let my hair go. I didn't think about going back in to tell my uncles. I just told her that she was stupid to think that I would steal money from Old People and I am not a thief. That maybe she would be the one that would steal if she had the chance. But I am not that kind of a person, and she was bleeding from the mouth. She went back into the bar, and I just walked away and went to the store.

I didn't even think of going back into the bar to tell my uncles what had happened. I just continued on and went to do my shop-ping. It wasn't until they were on their way home and I told them what had happened. But that didn't stop me from doing my duty to do shopping for them. I continued, and that was their wish too. They didn't want me stop. These people that are getting mad at me were the ones that never look at them. They never so much as say "Hello" to them. They said, "These people don't care about us Old People. You are the one that looks after us."

Another time, a niece of my uncle, Isaac Antoine's half-broth-er, his half-brother's daughter, came after me and she was going to beat me up, but someone was there this time and stopped her. When I told them about this, they said that they expected that to

Young Ruby weaving a basket, circa 1960s.
Courtesy of Molly Peter. Photographer unknown, 1960s (?).

PLATE I

Ruby dedicated this book in part to the five ladies who appear here and on the following pages: Theresa Thorne, Muriel (Molly) Hwuneem, Ellen White, Delores Louie and Violet Charlie.

Ruby's late sister Theresa Thorne (née Alphonse).
Courtesy of Molly Peter. Photographer unknown, date unknown.

PLATE 2

Ruby's late sister Muriel (Molly)
Hwuneem (née Alphonse).
Robert Daniels, date unknown.

Late Snuneymuxw Elder and
former Vancouver Island University
Elder-in-Residence Ellen White.
Courtesy of Vancouver Island University.
Photographer unknown, 2010.

PLATE 3

Ruby with her sister Delores Louie at Simon Fraser University's convocation
(2019). Delores was Ruby's best friend, strong support and colleague in teaching
and documenting Hul'q'umi'num'.

Simon Fraser University, 2019.

PLATE 4

Late Cowichan Elder and Hul'q'umi'num'
language teacher Violet Charlie.
Luschiim Arvid Charlie, 2001.

PLATE 5

Ruby's late beloved cousin Dennis Alphonse, who served
on Cowichan Tribes Council with her and was chief
for many years.
Courtesy of Molly Peter. Photographer unknown, 2004.

PLATE 6

Ruby with her late husband, Norman Spahan ("Cowboy").
Courtesy of Molly Peter. Pim's House of Photography, 2014.

PLATE 7

Family gathering (2014).

Courtesy of Molly Peter. Pim's House of Photography, 2014.

PLATE 8

With family backstage at the University of Victoria convocation in 2019, where Ruby received UVic's highest recognition—an honorary Doctor of Laws. *Sonya Bird, 2019.*

On floor: Kyla-lee Sxelu Hwuneem. Front row, left to right: Wayne Paige, Wayne Charlie, Bernadette Sam (Little Ruby), Leo Peter, Ruby, Delores Louie, Molly Peter, Adele Joe, Gerickah Peter. Back row: Ralph, Richard Daniels-Topaum, Susan Johnny, Paul Joe, Scarlette Hwuneem-Joe, Lynsey Hwuneem-Joe, Cameron Joe, Martina Joe, Brian Jimmy.

PLATE 9

Ruby at the University of Victoria convocation in 2019 with longstanding friend and Hul'q'umi'num' co-researcher Dr. Thomas (Tom) Hukari.
Sonya Bird, 2019.

PLATE 10

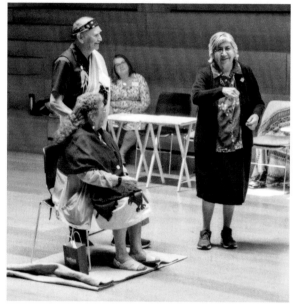

(*Above*) University of Victoria Honouring by the Department of Linguistics faculty and Dean of Humanities Dr. Lisa Surridge. Ruby was presented with a carved silver pendant of a Thunderbird, a symbol of power, protection and strength.
Chorong Kim, 2019.

(*Below*) University of Victoria Elder May Sam speaking at the UVic Honouring. May put down a blanket for Ruby in recognition of her high status, as is the custom. Hired speaker for the event Wayne Charlie stands behind Ruby.
Chorong Kim, 2019.

PLATE 11

Cowichan Honouring. Ruby addressing the guests, supported by daughters
Molly and Adele.
Shannen Joe, 2019.

PLATE 12

Great-grandchildren Darcy Joe III, Susannah Joe and William Paige
presenting Ruby with a blanket at the Cowichan Honouring.
Shannen Joe, 2019.

PLATE 13

Ruby with great-great-grandchildren (Adele's grandchildren)
Susannah, William, Laraleigh, Darcy III, Summer, Deven and
Paiten (in cradleboard) at the Cowichan Honouring.
Shannen Joe, 2019.

PLATE 14

Cowichan Honouring. Back row, left to right: Melissa (daughter),
Adele (daughter), Sheila (daughter), Leo (son), Charlie (grandson—Leo's son).
Front row: Molly (daughter), Delores (sister), Ruby, Bernadette
(Little Ruby—daughter).
Shannen Joe, 2019.

PLATE 15

Five generations of Molly's family. Front row, left to right: Molly Peter with Gracie, Ruby with Latisha. Back row, left to right: Shantel with Emily, Martin, Edie, Martina with Ava-Lynn.

Shannen Joe, 2017.

PLATE 16

Four generations of Adele and Darcy's family. Front row, left to right:
Darryl, Alana with Paiten, Darcy, Adele with Deven, Paul, Shannen, Anna-lee,
Darcy II with Violet. Back row, left to right: Summer, William, Laraleigh,
Darcy III, Susannah.

Shannen Joe, 2018.

PLATE 17

Ruby and Delores reviewing photos for *What Was Said to Me* at the Language House during our last working session in November 2020.

PLATE 18

Simon Fraser University awarded Ruby an honorary Doctor of Laws degree (2019) in recognition of her life's work to restore and teach the Hul'q'umi'num' language. Former president and Vice-Chancellor Andrew Petter does the honours. *Simon Fraser University, 2019.*

PLATE 19

Four generations graduating from Simon Fraser University. Left to right: Martina Joe (Ruby's great-granddaughter), Ruby Peter, Lynsey Johnny (Ruby's granddaughter), Bernadette Sam (Ruby's daughter). The Thunderbird design on the dresses was created by Ruby's father, Basil Alphonse, based on the family oral history. Ruby wanted her offspring to have a sense of belonging, as it is important to belong to your own family.
Simon Fraser University, 2019.

Simon Fraser University convocation. Ruby raising her hands in thanks after receiving an Honorary Doctor of Laws.
Simon Fraser University, 2019.

PLATE 21

Ruby's daughter Bernadette Sam's Royal Canadian Mountain Police graduation (1993).
Courtesy of Molly Peter. Photographer unknown, 1993.

PLATE 22

Ruby's parents, Cecilia Leo and Basil Alphonse, in 1972, just after Ruby and Ronald's family moved to their new house.
Courtesy of Molly Peter. Photographer unknown, 1972.

PLATE 23

Ruby preparing tule (the reeds of the bulrushes) for weaving mats at the Native Heritage Centre, Duncan, BC. Listen to Ruby speak about preparing tule at https://sqwal.hwulmuhwqun.ca/learn/tat-mustimuhw-life-in-the-olden-days/gathering-tule/.

Courtesy of Molly Peter. Photographer unknown, early 1970s.

PLATE 24

Daughter Sheila and Brant Johnny's traditional Big House wedding.
Courtesy of Molly Peter. Photographer unknown, 1972.

Ruby at Adele and Darcy Joe's wedding, with Adele's father, Ronald Peter.
Robert Daniels, 1982.

PLATE 25

Ruby with great-great-granddaughter Gracie Joe and great-granddaughter Keagan Wilson. "The Old People used to say you could talk to them (before they were born) and tell them things. Maybe they can't voice speak, but they can understand."
Courtesy of Molly Peter. Molly Peter, 2012.

PLATE 26

Late Ronald Junior's family. Left to right: Selena Peter, Rachel Henry, Maryellen Joseph, Michelle Sampson, Christine (Ronald's wife) and Heather Joseph, George Peter, Greg Joseph, Joanna Joseph.
Courtesy of Michelle Sampson. Photographer unknown, date unknown.

PLATE 27

Melissa's family. Back row, left to right: Marty, Chris, Jeremy.
Front row: Melissa, Eleanor and Leona.
Courtesy of Molly Peter. Photographer unknown, 2019.

PLATE 28

These four great-granddaughters from the Tsartlip
First Nation—Kaydence, Kaylin, Kloe and Keagan—
speak SENĆOŦEN, the language of the W̱SÁNEĆ on
Vancouver Island's Saanich Peninsula. They enjoyed
comparing words in SENĆOŦEN and Hul'q'umi'num'
with their great-grandmother.
Molly Peter, 2020.

PLATE 29

Bernadette (Little Ruby) Sam's family. Back row, left to right: Little Ruby, Tamra Sam, Joseph Sam, Susan Johnny. Middle row: Lynsey Johnny, Ruby Peter, Norman Spahan ("Cowboy"). Front row: Justice Hwuneem, Kyla-lee Sxelu Hwuneem, Nevaeh-lee Hwuneem. *Pim's House of Photography, 2014.*

PLATE 30

Ruby telling the Little Wren story during the 2015
Duncan Days with Little Ruby by her side.
Kyla-lee Sxelu Hwuneem, 2015.

A recording of Ruby telling the Little Wren story, learned
from her mother, can be found at https://saalhsqwal.
hwulmuhwqun.ca/ruby-peter-wren/. Courtesy of s'aa'lh
sqwal, a website of legacy stories presented by the
Hul'q'umi'num' Language and Culture Society.

PLATE 31

happened because they were jealous, but they didn't want me to stop helping them, because I was their choice and not these people that were just talking and getting mad.

It bothered me for just a very short while, and I thought about it, what my uncles were saying. That it was them, it was their decision of who can help them. I never thought, I never thought to ask for money or gas when I took them shopping. I left it up to them, and sometimes they would tell me, "You pull up to the gas station, and we will fill up your tank," or else they would ask if I had gas, one of them, they would kind of take turns. They'd either give me cash, if the tank was full then they'd give me cash and say, "Buy something for your children." They never said they were paying me; this was for the grandchildren, and I left it like that, the way they wanted it to be, and I never thought that I was wasting my time. I just enjoyed their company and loved listening to the stories they told.

I often wonder how I managed all the things that I did. By this time, I was in council. I was in different committees—education committee, land committee, adult education—and there was a meeting every night of the week. I was gone from seven. On Tuesdays it was until 11:30 p.m. During the weekdays: Tuesday, Wednesday and Thursday, seven until nine. Then the children that was—my own children, my foster children, the cattle, the Elders. And I seemed to have made time for just about everything that was going on around me. I guess it was just the help that I had from my parents that were always around me and assisting me. And Mother always said, "Someday your caring, your loving the Old People, it will come back." But I never waited for that. I never thought about it.

Then there was talk of getting a better house, that our house was too small, and then they were saying, "Try and get a new house." So we kept trying. Trying to get house. Right from 1950, and then it was about 1960-something, and then they, the Chief and Council, said they couldn't build on your land because your land is not settled. I knew I had a nest egg that I could—I didn't want to be far away from the land my dad gave me but was not really settled. So I was saying, "Well, maybe I could purchase a small little piece of land where the house can sit across the road." So I voiced my thoughts to my mother and when I talked to her, she usually talks to the others. Talks to the Elders. And I said, "I am willing to pay for, I have some money saved to pay for a small parcel where a house can sit. I don't want to be away from here, just across the road." So, I asked my uncle, I told him what I wanted. I just wanted a little piece, just enough for a house, a small little lot just enough for a house, where my house can sit, and that's all I want.

The next thing I knew there was discussions among the Elders, and then I was kind of pushed away. I was told, "OK, we're deciding," and I thought, "Who is 'we'?" Then I'd follow; when I followed, they told me, "Go back." I thought, "What is going on?" I looked out the window, and there was a councillor and there was somebody from Land Committee and my uncles were all there. I wanted to find out what was going on, so I stepped out of my house to go and ask, and I was shushed and told to go back inside: "You can't be included in this." And I heard my uncle talking— Little Joe—I heard him say, "I am the one that is deciding. You are not deciding, you are not deciding." He was pointing to these other relations, cousins, all the ones, Uncle Isaac and Simon and Grandpa. He says, "I am deciding, I'll decide what is going to be, what I want for her and for my grandchildren. It's not for the husband, it's not for any of you. This is for her and the children." To me, the tone that he used, the tone of his voice—just by listening I thought, "Oh, I better not go and interfere, I'd better move away, I better stay away. If I go closer, he will get angry at me." That is what I felt. So I went back, slowly back into the house. That wasn't my decision; it was his.

They left, and I was told, "You go cook, get something ready for the table." That seemed to be the thing to do for whatever was going on. If there was discussions going on, decisions to be made, that gets completed, and then you feed them, they eat. I got busy and started cooking and preparing the meal for when they'll come in—about an hour and a half, two hours later, they came walking in, and that's when I was informed. It was done. It was already—what they had done was measure. They got the Chief

124

and the Land Committee and they went measuring. I did ask my mother what they did, and she said she could not interfere either, "I just watched what they did. This is what they did. They measured. Your uncle walked from one corner, spacing his two legs out like a yardstick, and the way he walked he said that was about four feet, three feet. That was the measurement that was taken. From one post to the other, and he pointed where it was going to go, this is how far it is going to go, from that corner to this corner, and then on the frontage it was measured down to the west-side corner and then it was measure to the north corner, right along the fence."

And I said, "Oh, I just wanted a little for my house," and my mother said, "Shhhhhut up," in her Indian language. "Listen, listen to what your uncle is doing. This is for you, this is for the future, this is for your children. It is not for you and your husband; this is for you and the children." And I just—it wouldn't sink in. I just kept thinking, "I am a married woman, and what about him?" And she said, "No. No, this is for you and the children. You're the one. You're the one that has been with them. You're the one that did this, did that. You drove them, you shopped for them, you did everything they asked—you did. They are the ones that are deciding what they want to give you. You cannot interfere, you cannot talk, you cannot question it or say anything about it."

"Oh, my God," I thought. "Just accept it. OK, OK, I think I understand," and then I thought about what she had said to me before, that how you care for Old People, how you care for them, how you treat them, is how they'll treat you. But when he made the will, when he made it he said his claim was going to his niece because that was his wish, and niece and her children. So I just had to let it go at that and I thought, "Well, you have learned not to question anything, so this is another time you can't question your Elders at what they are doing or why they are doing it. This is their wish, and you have to accept it." So I accepted what was, what they had done. I thought, "Well, I guess I can't interfere, I can't have any say in this." It seemed it was a prediction from my Elders. It was really funny that they were so determined that I was, that it was my name that was going to be put on the land transfer, that the land goes in my name and only in my name and that it was going to be for the children.

I had no inkling at the time that there was going to be a marriage breakup or anything like that, but that at the time, that was what was said. And I really, my mind couldn't grasp it that that was what was being said. That if anything happens, then I would be left with nothing, and he did say it, he did say it. Uncle Joe did say it: "If anything does happen and the man decides, if I put it in his name, she'll be left with nothing. This way in her name that if anything happens with their marriage, she has the land, she has the children"; and it was determined there that I was going to keep the children, that I was going to have them, that will be for me and the children. And it's just so unbelievable. So that land was given to me, it turned out it was a little bit more than two acres, two, three acres of land that was given to me.

Twenty-two

A ND THEN NOT TOO LONG AFTER, my Uncle Simon, Simon Joe George, he was getting attached to my second son. They used to walk and talk together, and he was really getting attached to him. He turned around and told me, "I am leaving you land for my Charlie," because the name Charlie, came about really funny. With my son, we used to watch this Notre Dame soccer league. There were movies, and we used to watch almost every day. And there was this soccer player, and his name was Chuck Charles, and they called him Chuck. And that's where the name was picked up from. He used to watch this game, watch this movie every time it was on, just about every day, and he used to watch this. It became sort of an idol. He enjoyed watching that. So, when he went to school when he turned six, he started at St. Ann's School for Boys.

My boys all went to St. Ann's school—started at St. Ann's School for Boys. Junior went there, then Chucky started there, but then they built Queen of Angels. We moved them to Queen of Angels. I had a call from Sister Mary Sheila, the principal, who knew me very well, and she called and she says, "Ruby, do you have a son named Charles Peter?" And I said, "No, I don't have a son named Charles Peter," and I hung up on her after chatting for a few minutes. Then she called again and she said, "Are you sure?" I said, "No, my boys are, one is Benjamin, Benjamin Leo Peter; the other is Ronald Allan Peter." So I hung up again, and then the third time she called and she says, "This little boy insists that he is your son," and I said, "Describe him." So she described him, and I said, "Oh my God, that is my son. That's Leo Benjamin." "Well, how come his name is Chuck then?" I said, "Oh." I was stuck for words; I didn't know how to explain how come he was Chuck. He was given the name Chuck Charles Peter. It was completely different from his name, Leo Benjamin Peter. It was really funny; then finally I told her what he watched that Notre Dame, and because my uncle who was hard of hearing, he called him when they were walking, walking around. Chuck was always talking about his soccer player Chuck, and he started calling him Charles. "OK, you are going to be my Charlie," when they were walking, "You are going to be my Charlie."

And that is how he became Chuck when he started school at Queen of Angels. The name stuck on him. He has never been called Ben or Leo. Most of the time it has been Chuck. Only when he went to high school did he become Leo. Other than that, he was known by friends and relatives, known by everyone as Chuck. This was how much, how attached he was to his grandfather.[1] The children were all attached to him, especially Chuck.

When my uncle told me he was going to will him a piece of land, he said, "I am going to sign some land to you for my Charlie. It's going to be in your name, but it's going to be for your son." So the land is still in my name, and this is how this was another one of the Elders that I looked after giving me something to remember them by. I went with my uncle, and he brought me to Indian Affairs and he wrote it down. He made a will saying that his property, all the properties that he has, was coming to me. He just never had any children left. He had one son, Alfred, who died at the age of seventeen or eighteen or nineteen. I guess anyway, I guess I just sort of replaced something that was missing in his life, and we got sort of attached. He got attached to my children.

I guess it sort of proved the point that you care for your Elders and they care for you as well. That they look after them properly, take care of them, and there is always gratitude and they show it

---

1 In the Cowichan kinship system, a child would call a great-uncle by the term grandfather.

Ruby and her children (1967). Left to right, back row: Ruby holding Sheila, Alphonse, Darrin (foster child). Front row: Molly, Leo (a.k.a. Chuck), Adele, Ron Jr. Taken at Ruby's mother's home on Tzouhalem Road.
Courtesy of Molly Peter. Photographer unknown, 1969.

by doing some things for you. They don't just accept all the things that you do without doing something for you too. Giving—it's not just take and take and take and not give. It seems to work both ways. And I guess it just proves the point too what my mother had said to me, what she had stressed and her and dad were always talking about, how important it is to look after Elders and how to respect them, and that is what I did. I respected the Elders. I really, really cared for them. I didn't care what anybody thought. I never took anything from them. I never accepted money. I never asked them for pay and I never even asked them money for gas. For the transportation I gave, they were the ones that decided what was going to be. And if they gave me money, then I didn't—I couldn't say no to that either. But they never said, "This is for you." I never ever heard them say that I am paying you for what you are doing. They always said, "I would like to get something for my grandchildren." That was how it always went.

There were hard times. There were times that it was a really hard life. This was earlier on, when my older son, when my oldest son was a baby, and my dad's oldest son decided that, he didn't decide, he told us that there's a logging place, a camp, where we could stay and live in Olympia—no, Mount Rainier. And he said there was good money there. It was sort of a promise that the men can go to work logging and make money in three months and come home with lots of money. And being young and believing what we were told, that this was the truth, and it's there. So my brother and his wife, they had a child, myself, my husband and my oldest son, who was a baby then, and mother said, "I will keep your daughter; just take your baby."

So we went. We moved. And I thought, "Oh, we are going to make money, we are going to make lots of money, and the things we can do with it." We can help with the farm, we can help with this, and my mother believed in what she heard, too. We went across and stayed over in Mount Vernon. The job was not ready yet, so they brought us to a camp where they said they were going to take meantime jobs. So they went cabbage cutting. Every day they would leave early in the morning. At first, they came home with groceries and things that were needed in food and they brought home. They said, "Well, after two weeks we will go out to this camp."

The first week it was working out fine, but the second week—and my oldest brother, he had decided that he was going to drink. Then they started drinking, and the womanfolks were at camp, and there were no groceries, because we were living day by day, waiting for this logging camp to open up. And I was lucky that I was nursing my baby, but my sister-in-law wasn't. She was depending on milk because her baby was bottle fed. And the other sister-in-law had no children, so it wasn't so bad for her, but she had no groceries, and we were starting to get really worried. We thought something had happened to the menfolks. The imagination just sort of ran away and thought they had accidents, something happened.

At eleven thirty at night they came home—drunk, and no money, just beer cans on the car. This went on for three days. We were actually starving. The womanfolk were actually starving, and I was starting to get scared and I phoned my mother and told her what was happening. And she said, "Come home. Don't stay there." This was already October, November, something like that. September, October.

So I bundled up my baby and got on the bus and I had already felt sick. I told her I was feeling sick. The packing and carrying my baby—carrying my baby was really hard—and by the time I got to Victoria, my parents were already waiting for me, and it seems I just made it home. They took me directly to the doctor's office in Duncan, and the doctor examined me and told me, well, I had to be hospitalized right away because I had pneumonia. By then I was very, very sick, and my mother just took my baby. She already had my two older children. They phoned to Puyallup, to the camp where I left from, and informed them that I was in the hospital and that I was a very sick person. My husband came home and he had decided that he wasn't going back to the States; instead he looked for other jobs here at home.

It was two weeks later by the time I was released from hospital. My parents and the priests were always close by, and they helped us a lot with our problems because they thought it was becoming a problem. The alcohol was becoming a problem to my husband, and he eventually quit drinking and concentrated on working. And I got back into my routine, working at different homes as a homemaker. Most of them were part-time jobs which I worked with these people most of my life.

It was after my third child was about two, and we became foster parents. The child that was brought to me—two children—the mother died of heart attack. I knew the parents very well—Bob Thomas and his wife. Judy Ann Thomas became my foster child, she was two years old, and her little brother, Hoagie. And Hoagie was a beautiful baby, curly haired, smiling all the time. I had him for about, from about two months old, I had him for about six months. Judy was just turning two when we got her. She was about two-and-half years old. She was slow on getting her balance, on walking when she followed me because I used to get my water from outside and pack it in.

There was no indoor plumbing, no washing machine. We had a gas washing machine, and there was no Pampers. We had to wash our clothes, wash diapers and hang them out on the line. My everyday life was just that: washing, cleaning, going to work, coming home, cleaning up quickly; and there was always, from early morning to late in the evening, there was always something to do. My little foster child was getting attached; so was the baby. I kept my house spic and span because I was always leery about things on the floor—I had very limited toys for the children, and the older child used to pick up things up and throw them to the crib. So I was always watching her.

And then my mother-in-law was having a hard time. Her common-law husband beat her up really bad. She was really mistreated. Her asthma was really bad, so she moved in with us and then she injured herself on her arm and it festered. It was getting bad, and she didn't tell me right away. She said she was ashamed about letting me know she was hurt, that she felt like a child. I looked at her arm. And I always had medication around and I had this piece of white sheet. I always had some clean cloth, torn sheets, ready for use. So I took this little piece—it was about four inches wide and about ten inches long—and I gave it to her, I gave her the medication. I had no bandage, so I told her to use it as a bandage. I was very, very busy washing the clothes, washing the floor and cooking at the same time, and this was early in the afternoon, about three o'clock, two o'clock, something like that. I had given her the medication and told her I will help her later if she fixes it up. She put the medication on and she called me to tie it so I did. But I was so busy that I didn't even notice that the cloth I had given her—what she had done with it.

Then later on after supper, we noticed that my little baby, foster child, was coughing. I know he had a cough; it wasn't worrying me too much. It was a very slight cough. I looked at him, and he was sweating. I thought that was very odd, so I sponged him. I look at him again, and he was really breathing shallow and beads of sweat were all over his face. I really started to worry. His breathing was very shallow, so I just picked him up and said I am taking him to the doctor, taking him to the hospital; this was after hours of the doctor's office. I brought him to the hospital.

When they examined him, his temperature wasn't that high. They were starting to worry too. They couldn't get him to breathe properly, and I was really scared. I stayed there. They were telling me, "You can go home." I said, "No, I am not going home; I am going to stay with my baby. I am looking after him and I will stay with him." So I stayed right close. They put him oxygen, they did everything. And then suddenly he was getting worse. They thought he was going to die. I kept saying, "No, he can't." I said, "What is wrong with him?" They said they didn't know what was wrong with him. Then they sent me to call his father. They called the priest, and then they told me to go for Mr. Thomas. I went to pick him up and brought him back with me, and by that time, baby was really, really sick. He was really bad. They said he was not going to live through the night. I said, "What is wrong with him?" Mr. Thomas didn't want to wait. He just looked at his son and kind of shook his head and he said, "I am going home," and he left. I stayed there right by the bed, and then he started heaving, throwing up. So the doctor came over and the nurses and they turned him over, and he threw up.

When he threw up—and I don't know how they, they had moved me away—and what he threw up was really, really scary, and they took me aside and they asked me, questioned me again. What I was doing during the day, what I did. They asked me questions of all the things I did through the whole day, so I told them everything I did through the day, and then they showed me this piece of cloth. And I was shocked, looking at that little cloth. I said, "That is the cloth I gave my mother-in-law. She tore it in half and she used it on her arm." I didn't know what happened, but I eventually asked my mother-in-law; we had to question her too. She said she had put it beside her pillow, and we think that my little foster child, the two-year-old, got ahold of it and threw it in the crib where baby was. And that it happened. Poor little Hoagie. He ate that piece of cloth, and it choked him.

Oh, that was just so heartbreaking! It was just so terrible. He didn't live through the night. He was a newborn when we got him and he was about ten months when he died, because he was already starting to stand on his own two feet. And I used to tease him about showing off that he could stand.

The funeral arrangements I had to make. Mr. Thomas, he didn't want to take any responsibility. The loss of his wife and then baby. I always thought that he blamed baby for his wife's death. He said, "Do whatever you have to do, just leave me out of it." It was just heartbreaking to try and talk to him and the hurt that went with it, and those months that I had him, he became my baby. When you get attached to a child, you can't just throw him away and forget about him. That's how I felt. He became my responsibility, right to the time he died.

And Judy continued staying with us; she stayed with us until she was twelve years old. Then she was sent back to her father, which was very sad because he was an alcoholic. He was one of those people who were at residential school, and they lose all the teachings, all the things that we're supposed to learn from parents, and he didn't care about life anymore. And Judy, when they sent her back to her dad, she was twelve years old, and he was still drinking. And she thought I gave her up and threw her away, so she just joined her dad, and I lost track of her.

Many things happened. Judy was happy with me; she saw happiness in the home she was living in. But what happens to a child when they think that they're being thrown away and forgotten? When she was taken away from me, Indian Affairs said I wasn't to get in touch with her. I wanted to be still part of her life, to keep in touch with her, and they said no. They said that if I do, then I would be wrecking her life.

It wasn't only Judy; it was the other six children, the other six foster children that I had. Their mother was shot, and there was no one to take them, no one would take them because there were too many of them. I went to Social Services and the Band Council on the reserve to get them in a home, but no one would take them. They just kept telling me, "Two weeks, we'll find a place for them." Another two weeks and another two weeks more, and they eventually gave me ten dollars a month for each child for assisting me with food, because they said they were, because my husband was working, they were going to assist me with only ten dollars a month for each child. I was getting sixty dollars a month for the six children, which wasn't very much. So we struggled through all those years that I had all of them. The two children that was brought to me. I was getting sixty dollars a month for each of them. So it was hard making ends meet. The struggle we had with all the children. I just couldn't push them out of my house, because no one would take them.

By 1967 my health started to change, and I knew there was something happening to me. I was not sure what it was, but most of the time I was tired and feeling sick. Then we got word that we were going to get a house. My health started to get worse. So I went to the Band and asked for assistance. I told them that I was going to go to the hospital and will have to have an operation and will they assist me. That is all I was asking. By this time, I was attached to all these children, including my own. Fourteen children altogether, and I was asking the Band for a homemaker, just until I come out of the hospital. That is what I was telling them. I need someone to look after them—all fourteen children. For two weeks until I am on my feet.

Instead of helping me to cope with my problem, to assist me—they turned around and took all the children. The Social Welfare people had decided to return the children to the parents. When they did that, they told me that I could not contact them, I was not to talk to them, not to let them know what was going on, not to even speak to them, not to even get in touch with them, not to say hello to them. That was supposed to be a break—that I was not to contact them in any way. No notes; "just a clean break," they called it.

So they were all returned to their fathers. Each, all of these children, had only their father. So that is exactly what Social Welfare did. They returned them to their fathers. I tried telling them they can't do that because I knew all these people. I knew what was going to happen to the children, but they told me it was not my responsibility anymore: "You cannot contact them." I asked if they told the children that I was going into the hospital. They just kept repeating to me, telling, "They are not your responsibility." So I never did see the children, never talk to them for years.

Twenty-three

B Y THIS TIME, they were building our house. By 1968 they were building our house. This was after we were in a committee that was struck in 1965 and we worked with George Manuel, who was from Kamloops, and another person whom our committee called Squinius. We did a lot of work with the committee. There were about eight people, and Abraham Joe was our chairman. We used the media quite a bit and we tried to get funding for housing. We worked long hours. We had Abraham Joe as our chairman, myself, Dennis, Leonard Antoine, Andrew Tom, and my sister Muriel Joe was our secretary. There were about eight of us altogether who worked hard at what we were doing.

In the end, we did get funding for twenty houses. And this took about two years of hard work, two years of many, many reports of our people and the need of housing. We received monies for twenty homes. Five of these homes were for big families. Six bedrooms. Andrew, Tom, Leonard, Abraham Joe and Howard Jim received—oh, and Ronald Peter—each received a six-bedroom home, and only three of these homes were built on private land. One was ours and two were Howard Jim of Quamichan and Andrew Tom. We had to bargain to get our house. All the others received their house; they were built for them and paid for, and there wasn't much funding left, and they were talking about building us a small house. I said, "No, I want a big house." I guess maybe I was thinking about the children that were taken away, but I had decided that I wanted a six-bedroom house.

So the bargain was that in order for us to get a six-bedroom house, the house had to be built by ourselves. That they purchase the material, and then it was up to us to build the house. So we talked it over with everyone who we thought would help us how we were going to build it. Of course, my dad was right in there and Ronald Peter, Arvid Charlie, my late uncle Frances Joe George, and my son Ronald Peter Junior. They got to work and they started building the house in 1968. They had very little carpentry experience. My dad had built a house with his father, so he was kind of guiding, helping, and the children's father had done carpentry in school, so that helped.

The house took exactly two years to build. The material that was purchased was $8,900 for the material. The hydro, the plumbing and furnace, and it came to a total of, I think it was $18,000 altogether. By 1972 the house was completed. I was so happy about that. Six bedrooms, big rumpus room, big living room, big kitchen, and I was always working, so I went out of my way trying to get the best I could get with what I was earning. I got a big kitchen table. Oak kitchen table with chairs that I paid $280 for. I got some chesterfield sets that were very nice, and I have this cabinet that I have had for years and years. I brought that up. It's got a little cupboard, and I keep pictures on it.

Things went along fine for a time, and then the drinking started again. My health wasn't too good. The tests that were going on for the past two or three years was just coming to a head. Then in 1970, they told me that I had cancer and that I had to go for an operation. And at that time, we were already living in our new house. I went to town and got groceries, and then discovered I was stranded in town, so I took a cab home. Getting home, I found the adults with drums in their hands and I asked what was going on, and then I looked and my son was crying, and I said, "What was going on?" "Oh, we are going to sing his song,[1] we are going to sing his song." And I said, "No, no, you can't do that. You're not going to do that to my son." That is what got them angry. I took the drums from everybody else, and because I did that, I got a punch

---

[1] His spirit song.

in the mouth. I fell on the floor and fainted. Someone phoned my parents because somebody was picking me up and my mother was driving in and my mouth was bleeding so bad. We filled it up with cotton, and it wouldn't stop bleeding, so I went up to the hospital and I had eighteen stitches inside my lips.

Then my parents knew that I was supposed to go into the hospital, and then my brother heard what had happened and he was very upset. He doesn't usually do the deciding of any major decisions, but when he heard what happened, he just told our mother that "enough is enough." What he said was, "I don't want her buried. If we don't do something, the next thing we will be doing is burying my sister. I don't want that." And he said, "Put her in the Longhouse, put her in the Big House. Get her away. She is not a pauper—she belongs to too many things. You can't let them do that to her."

My mother carried out his wish because he had decided and she had to carry out that demand from my brother. The funny part is that she had promised me, in all those years, she always told me she didn't want me to become a dancer. "I don't want you in the Longhouse, I don't want you to be a dancer. Your brother, yes, but not you." She told me, "I will never put you in the Big House, I will never make a dancer out of you," because I was never a dancer.

So I thought that was going to be kept. I thought I would never end up in the Longhouse. I never had anything against the Longhouse. I always thought someday I would go, because my mother said she would never put me in there. It would never happen. But when I realized that she was going to put me in the Longhouse, I got scared. I was afraid and I knew that I was sick. They all knew that I wasn't well, but they were more afraid of me dying in somebody else's hands.

It is a hard thing to understand; it is a hard thing to make clear what it means. To me, I was put in the Longhouse because I was being mistreated and because of my high standard as a Native person, of what we hold, because we are from the Thi'tha. We help the people, and people come to us for help for many things. For funerals, for after funerals, for the Longhouse, for honouring of the deceased people, the Rattler, we hold all those, and that is considered high status, and this was the reason I was put in the Longhouse. Not to be disciplined, but because of the highest respect my parents and my brother had for me. Because of what they felt that I was the most important person and being abused wasn't part of that. And that is what they told me when they put me in the Longhouse.

I was angry, yes, I was angry. I was upset because I was being taken away from my children and I knew I couldn't talk to them. I couldn't converse with them. I could see them but I couldn't converse with them, and that is what upset me. And I knew that they put me in the Longhouse because of the greatest respect for me, the love they had for me, but I still felt anger of the separation from my children.

But that was short-lived after the four main days. The four main days I didn't eat. I was given tea, I was given broth, and I didn't know night and day; I didn't know it was daybreak, just that things happen at daybreak, and you have to keep still, obey all the rules; and that is the most important part in the Longhouse, is the obedience of the teachings. And because I heard my mother preaching to those that go to the Longhouse that I know what I was representing in there. Even though that my mother was the person, I still had to learn things, more experience than I have ever had.

I guess it must have fulfilled all the things that you wonder about when you find the answers to what you were wondering about, and that is what happened to me. I got all the answers about the life in the Longhouse and separating it from your life at your home. The different things that happen between the two different lives—then deciding the difference between the two. Why they call it the beginning for a dancer, and it just made me realize more of the important things I hold in life and the reason why my mother chose me to carry and for the people to understand and for me to be able to carry it and to open it to the people, to show them, to make them understand things about life in the Longhouse.

I didn't hold any grudges against anybody after, and they knew that I wasn't well so I was in the Longhouse for only three months, and the three months was really hard. The three months that I was in there almost totalled my life because of the action, the running, the staying up late, the travelling, because we travelled from one Longhouse to another Longhouse, going for a bath early in the morning, dancing and then going to another Longhouse, whether it was on the Island or on the mainland across the States. There was constant travel, constantly going. And who transported me? My parents. They didn't talk to me to the extent, because that was one thing that I was taught. You don't converse with no one. "You don't converse with me, you don't converse with your dad, you concentrate on your being. This is for you and you alone. Nobody else," and that is exactly what I had to do. That I had to be there only for me and that I could not converse with no one.

I saw my children. My little ones, my baby. They were allowed to sit in front of me. Shyly look at me and look away from me, in case I see their smiles, but they could not talk to me. That was an interesting three months. My oldest son became the daddy for looking after the children. He became rebellious, just for a short while. He was the cook, he was the one that got the children up, got them dressed. He looked after the baby, the little ones. He was rebellious just for a short while, and my mother was so good at talking that he came to understand what they were doing for me was for my own good and for theirs. I guess that is part of the reason that saved me from insanity. It saved me from losing myself or doing something to myself. I think it really helped me.

Late May when I was totally released from the Longhouse Thilelum' and I was allowed to go home. And I thought, "Well, maybe things will work out in my marriage," because it was on the rocks. "Maybe things will change," because he had come to the Longhouse and I was forced to talk to him by one of the dancers and I was called outside, which wasn't supposed to happen, and my mother and father were gone. They went to get groceries for the children and check up on them and left me alone at the Longhouse. I had no babysitter,[2] and the one that was there called me outside and said, "Your husband wants to talk to you, you go out

---

2 In this context, a babysitter is a caretaker of the initiates in the Big House.

there and talk to him." She said that in a commanding voice, that I had to do it. I told her, "No, I don't want to." She said, "No, you listen, you go out there and talk to him." So I reluctantly went out and didn't know what to say; I just stood there and just felt like crying, and just then my parents drove up. They drove up close to where I was standing. Of course, Mother was totally upset and asked me what I was doing. I didn't answer and it was later on when I told her what happened—all that I ever heard him say that he was sorry. I don't remember anything else.

After I came home, I thought things were going to be better. I thought things would improve. This was going towards summer time. And to my disappointment, the weekend came along and I still thought that we were going somewhere, thinking that we were going shopping or somewhere special. To my disappointment, we ended up at the liquor store with some people getting on the car. And then driving around, going to the Mariner's Pool, getting forced to drink. Beer was handed to me, and I was commanded to drink this, and I said, "No, thank you." "Who do you think you are? Goody two shoes, too good for your friends now. You think you are too good," and I thought, "Well, here comes the fists," so I put the beer to my mouth and pretended to be drinking.

That stopped the language abuse. I started a conversation, anything to get out of the abuse—trying to make jokes. I said it was hot out, so I opened the door, and while everyone was talking, laughing, I spilled the beer. Pretended I was drinking again and handed the can back and was given another can. I did the same thing again.

Then they talked about jumping into the water, and it was hot, it was already hot. So I went and sat on a big boulder rock. They all got off and they were laughing and talking and all of a sudden, I was scooped up. "You are going to go for a swim!" I said, "No, thank you!" and struggled, but I couldn't get out of it. And he jumped into the water and I screamed, "I don't know how to swim." I was just screaming my head off, "I don't know how to swim! I don't know how to swim!" While I was screaming, "I don't know how to swim," I was pushing him under the water because I was so mad, so angry that I was going to teach him a lesson. Put him under water, every time he came out, I'd start screaming, "I don't know how to swim! I can't swim, I can't swim!" and I would push his head under the water with both hands. And I would let him go, and he would surface up, and I'd start screaming that I didn't know how to swim and I would push him under the water again. I thought, "Gee whiz! I am going to drown him!" because I noticed he was having a hard time, struggling, so I paddled, I swam ashore. And he was still choking in the water, and I was already climbing up the shore, and somebody helped him get out of the water.

It must have been hot enough because my clothes just got dry, just dried out, and they were just playing around and having a good time, and that was the day that I was supposed to go the hospital for my operation. After about lunch time, after lunch, about twelve thirty, one o'clock, we started driving again and came to Koksilah and came to the amber light, and that's really funny, I guess it was noticed that I wasn't getting drunk or something. I don't know what was going on, why he was persistent that I drink. I was handed another beer. I said, "No, thank you," so I got booted out of the car. The door was opened, and I was kicked right off—physically kicked with his foot—and I fell off the car. I was still sitting there, and the car drove away. And I thought, "Well, that didn't matter. It was all for the best that I was kicked off." I felt hurt but I thought, I was always thinking of my children. Thinking what would happen to them if I don't go for what I am supposed to, for the operation, and I already heard what was happening to my foster children, the children I had. And that was the same people too that were keeping company with the children's father—they were drinking together.

So I walked from there to the hospital, Cowichan District Hospital. I didn't call anybody. I just thought, "Just do it!" So I walked all the way to the hospital. I got in there and registered and admitted myself. I was put into a room and I was getting prepared for the operation for the next morning. He must have guessed that I went to the hospital, because by four o'clock I had a visitor, and: what was I doing in the hospital? "There is nothing wrong with you, you get out of that bed and you come home!" I was to be dragged out of the bed and dragged home, but the nurse ran out and got some orderlies, and he was dragged out of the room. The doctor ordered for no visitors.

I had my surgery the next day. Major operation, and my good Dr. Pawlowski was very concerned. He was very glad I was going for my operation, but he was concerned about the children and their safety, and praying that I would come through it and he would get all the cancer out. That is exactly what he said to me before I went under anesthetic. He said, "I am putting this syringe into your vein so you will go to sleep in ten seconds, so you better say your prayers that everything will be alright after, that we can get all the cancer out."

That is exactly what I did. I said my prayers and I woke up. When I woke up after, my parents were there. I was lucky. They were always beside me; they were always there. Ten days later, I went home to the children. I had a lot of cattle, so Mom and Dad decided shortly after that, after I was on my feet again, they decided that I was going to separate from the marriage, the father of their grandchildren. I didn't want to admit that it was no go, it was no good. I guess I kept thinking that maybe he'd smarten up. After I got on my feet, I was kept under observation by the doctors. I was being watched for at least five years, and the children's father wasn't hardly home any more. He was already going somewhere else with someone else.

Twenty-four

I WAS WALKING TO TOWN, I was going to go for some groceries, and it was summer time, a very warm day, and my mother came along and she says, "Get on." I said, "Um, Mom, I want you to take me to the store." I wasn't really listening to her; I was just telling her what I was going to do, and she said again, "Get on." So I got on the car. I repeated what I was saying: "I am going for groceries. Would you take me to the grocery store for your grandchildren?" And she says, "It is already done. I already went to the store. I brought some groceries for your house. I have all the groceries at your house. I bought a lot." I said, "Mom, I am going to the store." She says, "No, we got called to go somewheres." I said, "You got groceries already?" She says, "Yes, I got groceries," "OK."

As soon as I said, "OK," she knew that she had me, that I had agreed to whatever, that I was going along with whatever her plans were, and then she tells me, "We are going away." "Where are we going?" I asked. "We are going to Kamloops," she said. "Kamloops!" She said, "Yes, we got called to Kamloops." I said, "Mom." She said, "Ah-ah, I already told you I arranged it." And I was going to ask about a babysitter, "Your father is going to stay with the children; the groceries are all there. They are going to be fine." I was just going to ask for a babysitter, but I couldn't: she already had a babysitter all arranged. So what can you say?

So I thought, "Well, I haven't got no luggage, I haven't got a coat, I haven't got a suitcase." I said, "I haven't got anything." She said, "Oh, that's fine, that's OK, dear. We will fix that in a little while." "Where are we going now?" "We are going to pick up Ray Peters, your nephew Ray and his wife, and we are going through Vancouver. I will pick you some clothes up over there." And that's her way, that was her way of not hurting the children and not hurting me from leaving the children. She had her own ways of solving things or trying to help with something. Her way of trying to get me out of the rut, the depression, the hurt.

So we went to Vancouver, and she took me to store and bought me clothes and shoes, and whatever else I needed, she was going to get it. She wasn't exactly poor, she always had money somewheres; put away for emergencies, as she called it. I guess I was her emergency. When she needed the money and she wanted me to go with her, she took out her money. She made sure that I was—that I had the right things.

So we travelled to Kamloops. We were gone for just about a whole week. We left in the afternoon and we stopped in Mission, then we travelled again, and along the way Ray Peters was driving. Mom and I were in the back, and she tells Ray that "along the way if you see water that is falling from the mountain, you stop." I thought, "Oh, my gosh! Now what is going on?" and I thought, "Oh, my gosh! I am going to have to go for a bath," and well, I didn't really mind that if I had to. I didn't say anything, I didn't comment.

So Ray was driving along and he saw this waterfall and just kind of steep and he says, "There's waterfall." "OK, stop the car," mother demanded. "Stop the car right now." He pulled over real fast and then he, Ray Peters, telling us, "I guess you women have to go for a bath." Mother answered him, "No, women can't bath with a man, so you go for a bath. We women will wait for you on the car." He looked at her and frowned at her, and then I guess he thought, "I guess, she's my Elder; I better quit this frowning." And she asked him whether, if he was chicken. What did she say in Indian now? "Are we going to be embarrassed about you being a man, that you aren't going to go for a bath?" "Oh, I'm going, I'm going, I'm going." That was a quick answer coming from him. He had to go skinny dipping and he went down to that hill, it was quite a ways, and not too long after, he got back. "Yep, the water was cold, but it was very good." So he did that twice before we reached Kamloops. It was really nice over there. We really enjoyed it, except that it wasn't a Native that we brought in: it was a hwunitum (white person) we had to bring in to honour. She—my mother—had a different song for that white person. There are different songs for the white person; there's different songs for different occasions, so she had one for him, for that occasion. After just about a whole week—we were there about four days—and we came home. We really enjoyed our stay.

The real purpose of that trip, for taking me along to work with her, was to separate me from the children's father, who was going around with another woman, and she and the Old People didn't like me being abused and they wanted me to separate, which I wouldn't accept because I felt that "for better and for worse." But the Old People had already decided that they were trying to save me from the abuse and the children were to stay with me. When we were coming home, when she told me, when she had me by myself and she starting talking to me and telling me the importance of life and that I should let him go. When we did get home, he was already living with another woman. Her first thoughts were my safety and the children's. The worry she had was my little ones would be fine; the older ones would have to become more important. To keep them busy, to talk to them, to make them understand what was happening to the marriage. And they were very patient with the children, and it was true about the older children. The teenagers, they were the ones that took it hard.

I was so glad there was cattle to fall back on, and Dad taking over the children and having them participate in sports, canoe races. And their education became very important. They helped me with all of that. Making sure the children were in school and making sure they participated in the canoe races.

My dad was a canoe paddler. They had canoes. My grandfather, Alphonse George, was a canoe builder. So Dad had canoes that they made use of, and the children, the teenagers, really worked hard to become champions. He told them what to do, he went with them, and I travelled with the children. Mother stayed home with the little ones, but they seemed to become very close to us in helping me with the children. All of them, both boys and girls, my oldest daughter, Leona and Junior, Chucky, Molly—they all became canoe-race pullers. The little ones, Ruby, Adele and Sheila, they were very small, and Alphonse was ten years old, so he was in between and eventually became a paddler. But the practice was very intense—they did a lot of running, a lot of practice in the water with an eleven-man canoe. They had to pull buckets of water. Throw a bucket in the water and pull that. It makes the canoe very heavy when they tow buckets. They used to run from Quamichan to Cowichan Bay, and a lot of other teenagers became interested in the canoe races and became champion for many years. Making St. Michael canoe champion, also Lady Esther and Mount Prevost.

I more or less concentrated on the children after our marriage broke up. In 1970, I was hired by Indian Affairs. I was the coordinator for the adult education. I used to have night classes for the Elders. I also was hired by Indian Affairs to teach the language, and when I did—that must have been in '71—I wasn't very happy with what I was doing, because I was just doing verbal and actions in teaching the kindergarten, grade one, teaching them running, standing, sitting down; action words—that was what I was doing. There was no writing in our language; it wasn't written, and this really disturbed me, so I kept telling my mother, telling her, telling my parents that I didn't like what I was doing.

In '72, she said we ought to do something about it. So my sister, Delores Louie, and myself. I wasn't going to be alone travelling. I asked my sister to come along with me and told her we were going to see all the colleges and school districts and talk to them. That must have been late in '73, because by September 1973 we had a class going. We travelled from Duncan, Chemainus, Nanaimo, to Victoria, Camosun College, UVic. We couldn't get anywhere, so we went to Camosun College and we heard about NITEP[1] and a Mr. Armstrong. We met with him and told him what we wanted. What I was doing earlier, that I was teaching and that I wasn't happy. They kept throwing questions at us: "What do you want to do about it?" I said, "Well, the language is not written; it is not in any

---

1 Native Indian Teachers Education Program, University of British Columbia.

kind of writing system." Then he said, "How about the Linguistics Department? I know someone there." So he called the head, dean of the Linguistics Department. And Mr. Warkentyne called us to go and see him. So we went to see him, and Mr. Armstrong came along, and all in that day we met with different kinds of teachers. Richard (I forgot his last name), he was in there, and then they all got together and discussed it and they decided that something was going to happen. A diploma program was going to go. That is what they told us.

They told us to find at least six people to apply, and they were going to get the other four. We got busy and we started to see people that we thought were interested in developing the language or learning how to do the writing system. We were quite successful. We had Ellen White and Violet Charlie, Delores, my late sister Muriel, Theresa Thorne, and we brought their names. By September we had a class going for the language.

Twenty-five

I WAS DOING KNITTING, knitting a bit of sweaters at the time, and my sister and I decided to go to Vancouver. We were called to Vancouver. We had three sweaters each. We didn't know how to sell it. We ran into someone we knew from strawberry times, a long time ago, and he said, "I know a place to go where we can sell crafts and sweaters. I will bring you there." So we followed him, and that is how we sold our sweaters. And his brother was there, who I never met before. I knew Joe from way back since we were very young. He used to go strawberry picking with us. We used to go to the same camps, but I never met his older brother. I knew there were a lot of brothers and sisters. That is how I met his brother, Norman Spahan.

He started phoning me. He asked for my number, and I told him I didn't have a number, so I gave him my mother's number. And he started phoning to Cowichan, to my mother's place. She would come down to my place and tell me, "Oh, there's a call for you, and he is going to call back in a while." So I would go to her house and wait. Then I wasn't really interested, not at first. My mom must have been talking to him quite a bit. It was until quite a while later before I found out that there was a lot of conversation between my mother and Norman, and he was calling just about once a week. And then after a few months he said he was going logging, so I thought that meant he was losing interest, so I was just kind of thinking that there was no interest, it didn't mean anything.

My son was going on a trip; he already had a child. He had a wife, and we were all living together, and he said, "I will take you along with us, Mom." He was already a working person. So he took me along for a trip, and we were in Seattle. We were getting on the Space Needle and we were getting ready to go up, and I said to my son, "Grandma is going to be angry I haven't phoned her." This was the second day we were there. He said, "Here's some money. You go and phone her."

I ran to the phone and phoned home, and my mother said, "My goodness, I have been waiting for you to call me." "Mom, what is the matter? Is something wrong?" "No," she said, "but get home right away." I said, "What do you mean 'get home right away'?" She says, "There is somebody coming over to see you, and you are way over there. You get home right now." I said, "Mom, who is coming?" She just kept getting frustrated with me that I was far away, and I finally agreed with her, and she told me who it was. I told her, "No. He said he was going to be gone, he was going up north to Alaska to work." She said, "Never mind what he said. He is coming over. You come home."

So I agreed to come home and I went to my son and told him, and my son said, "I will bring you to the ferry and you can go back." Go back through the Seattle ferry through to Victoria, but the ferry was on strike. I thought, "Oh, well, there goes." And I kept thinking about mother and how angry she was. I thought, "Well, I better try something," so I talked to this lady, and this lady said, "We are all stuck; we're stranded here. We have no way of getting anywhere, but I have a friend. I am going to talk to her. If we can pool our money, maybe we can hire her to bring us to Port Angeles and we can catch a ferry from Port Angeles to Victoria." So I agreed with this, and the lady agreed, so we all jumped on her station wagon and we came through Port Angeles from Seattle, and all pooled our money and all gave her money for the trip. I got to Victoria, and Norman Spahan was there waiting for me. He was just window shopping.

My parents met him, and they seemed to get along quite well, and he has been with us ever since 1973. My dad got along with him, and he was a rodeo man so he knew about cattle, cattle ranching, and he just came into the family and started helping my dad, doing things with him, helping with the cattle. Then he didn't want to travel. He just absolutely refused to go anywhere. Every time I mentioned about going somewhere, he said, "I did all my travelling. You can go with your children to go to the sports because I have done all my travelling and I am going to stay here." And that is just what he did, he stayed home with my parents and helped them with the farm work and looking after the cattle; because every day my dad was feeding the cattle, which was about sixty head by then, and he felt that the need was more important at home than to be with me and the children, who were already going into their adulthood.

By this time, I was already starting to feel that I should start thinking about myself, about my life; and the children were already old enough—they were young adults and they were starting to tell me that I should start thinking about myself. They knew that there was another person in my life. He was a very quiet man and he never forced himself on the children to be liked by them. They just sort of automatically turned to him whenever they needed to talk to someone, and my dad got along with Norman so well that I couldn't believe it. Just watching him and Norman walking around and talking together; it was something to see the attachment between the two of them.

My dad was already aging; his age was starting to show. We were already all starting to notice that both of my parents were starting to age, look tired. They were in their seventies by then. As my parents were starting to age, they started talking about how someday they were not going to be around, and the teachings became a little more intense. They had slowed down in going to the Longhouses and different places, and it seemed that a lot of Elders were starting to die off and they started to think about what was going on around the concerns that they had about the people. Not only their grandchildren and their children, but the people around the valley. About the teachings and how people—what was happening to our people. The worry they had about them, all around the things that had happened and the things that should come back. They had noticed the difference between a long time ago and what had happened. How the Masks were taken away from our Native People and the potlatch was stopped.

The potlatch was a do that went on for days—four days to one week. You would have people come around and stock up on food, different kinds of foods, then have a big do for four to five days, even to one week, and people would be around all that time for different things that would go on. This wasn't in the winter time. This was in the summer time, and people used to come around from all over. Mother used to talk about, we used to hear both of them talking about, answering each other, about how they used to have potlatch and how many Longhouses there were in Quamichan, and people used come and visit in those great big canoes, q'xhuw'lh, and they would stay for days and days participating in this potlatch. And there would be different things going on in all that, in all those days they were having it. The feast—the people that were visiting in those days, they were given breakfast, dinner and supper. And places—they had Longhouses all over the Cowichan area, that they would sleep in all these different Longhouses. There were thirty-six Longhouses in Quamichan by itself. There were as much as five hundred people at one time, and they used to have the do go on for different people would be putting the potlatch on.

There isn't so many pictures. There's only pictures of Shlamus and Hwuneem, who was our grandfather. Joe Jim's father was shown throwing blankets away to people and then putting down a bale of goat blankets to other families that are going to have a potlatch too, and when they do that, they will tie up a whole bale of maybe ten blankets and then lower it down to the next person that is going to have a potlatch, and that person would owe this person ten blankets for—that's how they helped each other.

It still happens this day, but not as, not like the way they used to have it long time ago. That it used to carry on. It's only over-night now; it's not like the way it was when they carried on for almost a week. But these were people that came were from all over the Island and as far as USA and Mission that would come and visit and stay for days. And West Coast people still have that. Just recently, that was two or three years ago, that I went to one, and that was on for three days, Thursday, Friday, Saturday, and we

Quamichan Potlatch blanket toss (between 1890 and 1900). Shlamus, Joe Jim's father, and Hwuneem, Ruby's grandfather, throwing blankets away to people and then putting down a bale of goat blankets to other families that are going to have a potlatch.

RBCM Indigenous photo collection. Photographer unknown, between 1890 and 1900.

came home Sunday, Sunday afternoon. And they had it in—their Longhouse was not that big, but it held quite a number of people.

And that was a very interesting experience to see, and this is something like we used to have. But ours was stopped by the government in the 1800s, and our people were threatened jail terms if they didn't give up their Masks and Rattlers and different things that they used for the potlatch, the things that they did. So the government confiscated a lot of Masks, a lot of Rattlers and baskets and different things that were used and have never been returned to our Cowichan people. So the potlatch was stopped, and Indian dances was stopped, and a lot of our people went underground, but Indian dance were carried on secretly for a number of years. Our Indian dance is the only thing that is holding our young people together as Native People. They're lost from residential school and they feel lost because their identity was taken away from them.

A lot of the people were in residential school from the time they were six years old until they were thirteen, or from nine years to sixteen before they were released. A lot of them lost their language. Some of them didn't even, don't even know their identity, their background, their ancestors, their names, their Indian names. The things they belong to. A lot of them lost their language totally and have no identity, and the Longhouse winter dance is the only thing that is holding them as recognizing themselves as Native People. This is just like a thread that they are hanging on, and they are trying so hard to get their Indian ways back. And I know that the language is part of the problem. I realized that a long time ago, and that was part of the reason why I wanted to do something about the language, tried so hard to get it back, and I know what my people are going through. Seeing them suffer and seeing how lost they are, how they have lost their identity of where they come from.

When I say, "where they come from," meaning to know they belong to something special. Their Indian name, where their Indian name came from, and this is something that we have been looking at and tracing, and even the treaty group have been looking into different things, and it is hard that a lot of the young people don't know where they come from. Their parents who were in residential school were just totally lost: they had no teachings, nothing to tell their children. The history of Indian names is very important to our Native People. It tells them where they are from, what they belong to, which side of the family holds whatever work that goes on in the Native community, and some of our people do or have traced their Native names to as far as Yakima, USA, and some to Regina and Squamish. Indian names are very important.

The only teachings that is being held is the Longhouse, the winter dances. This is the only thing that we have left. And with our young people that are trying to look for something, we have advised to them to go into the kitchen of the Longhouse, where the teaching is told everyday throughout the winter. We have advised some people to go to the Longhouse to listen to the teachings—young people who are in trouble—and they have felt that this was very helpful to them.

We often hear the leaders and young people talk about wanting to get the old teachings back because they feel that some of the teachings are just made up by some of the leaders, and they always say we want to get the old teachings back. They have talked to me about it and have come and approached me about what they are being told and what some people have made some things that aren't true. And we have had to separate the ones that aren't the real teachings and tell them, "Well, this is the real one; you have to follow this one." Some young people think they are being told something that aren't really, really true—teachings that wasn't from a long time ago.

They are right. Some of the teachings that did come up that I heard, which have been corrected, were just made up. So the leaders are starting to get together and talk about what is the correct way of correcting all the old teachings alive and how to go about it. And I believe talking about it is the most important and approaching Elders that know the teachings to confirm which is the proper teachings; and I think this is happening now to the young people in the Longhouses. They have been going to the Elders and talking to them.

And the other thing that they asked me about was, what can the Sxwuyxwi be used for? What is the proper way, what proper way to use them for, when is it proper to use them? My response was, the Rattler and the Sxwuyxwi are almost identical. The Rattler is just a rattler that is in your hand, the Sxwuyxwi is the mask on the people's face that belongs to it.

And it's only certain people that belong to the Rattler and to the Sxwuyxwi. They have to be a descendant of the people that belong to it. The Sxwuyxwi, the one that wears the Mask, can perform marriages, funerals, picture memorials, and they used to have a baby cradle song for a baby to be rocked. Puberty, when a young lady first changes her life, and they had a do for her at the fourth day, people cleansing when somebody gets hurt, something happens to someone and then you have the Mask Dancers brush them. Naming—they can do the naming, to receive a Mask, bathing new dancers, those are the same things that the Rattler can do. Anyone from the Rattler can do, except for the bathing new dancers. That is something they can't do, the Rattler people can't do. But they can do the hair, combing of the hair, special way of doing the hair.

And people that are from Thi'tha, the ones that belong to the Rattler are called Thi'tha. They are very special people and they would have to be a descendant from the Rattler; and they burn, they can do burning of food, burning of clothes, starting new life, or using sharp things—there's songs for that. Sharp things as axe, knives, needles, scissors and paddle, guns. And it's a separate thing to do seafood. There's different these things like fish and clams. There's songs for all of these, different songs, and this is something that many of our people have lost: a lot of them were Thi'tha. Because they were raised in residential school, they have lost it completely. There are some that are trying to find their way back into that. Some of them are looking for their Masks, which was taken away from their ancestors.

Their Indian name usually helped. The history, traditions, where the name came from, their background, whether they held the Rattler, the Mask Dance. There was always something that told them of who they are. But the ones that went to residential school: if they spoke their language, they were whipped, they were punished severely; and when they came out, they had lost their language. There was no teachings behind them, because they were taught the English language and they were just lost in the two worlds: their Native World, which they lost, and then the White World, which was new to them. They had no inkling of who they were, and it is really sad that when they had children, they didn't even really teach them anything. They just sent their children to school—they didn't tell them anything. Some tried, some just totally gave up and some of them still have their nightmares of what they went through in the residential school. Not only the residential school, but the day school. It was really hard on everyone. It was only those that had parents that were fluent that still kept the language, the teachings, still hanging on to some of the traditions. But so many—too many—lost out on the traditions and teachings.

These are all the things that are my concerns as well as my late parents'. They were concerned about all these things, even the funerals. They were concerned about it because they were saying that when someone dies, they have to be buried on the fourth day, and everything was in fours. You bath for four days after you lose someone and then you abstain from alcohol, smoking, for the rest of the year. And even the new dancers have to abstain from alcohol and smoking for the year. Get away from bad habits. This was really stressed to me that this had to be done, that this is very, very important and that our children have to know this; they should remember that there is a new beginning for people when they have a change of life, puberty, when they become a dancer, when they become orphans, when one parent dies. These are all the times for them to follow rules in order to have a better life for themselves. This was very important and very stressed to me, to watch my children, to remind them to make sure that they know all these things.

Twenty-six

WHEN I WAS GOING TO SCHOOL, I stayed at UVic until 1978 because of my interest in linguistics. I did part-time in assisting Professor Hukari in teaching at UVic. I really enjoyed that time. These were non-Indians we were teaching, and it was very interesting, an interesting year. And all this time my mother helped me with my children who were becoming adults by that time. In the seventies, my older children were looking after the younger children, but my mother was always around. Even though she was getting sick—she had heart condition—and she didn't want to keep still. She backed away from everyone, the Longhouse, and my dad stayed with her, but she never stopped coming down to my place to be close to her grandchildren. In 1974 we were told that she didn't have very long to live, and she passed on in 1975 when she died. And then I felt that my mother had fulfilled all her wishes—that she had wanted a lot of grandchildren and she always told me that she wanted a lot of great-grandchildren. I think it made her really happy that there were a lot of grandchildren, um'imuth, and that was her pride and joy to see them grow up, to see them win all those trophies they had when they were canoe pulling. I think that made her and Dad the happiest in all their life, and then as my children were getting married, she was always there.

My daughter, when she was at Malahat, she had two children in Malahat and then she came home after her marriage broke, and she came home and she got married again. She had boys.

My oldest daughter, she passed away in 1977 and left behind two beautiful children, one whom I raised, Melissa, and the boy, who my second-oldest daughter raised. But I always told my children, "Your grandma will be very proud of you. Maybe she's gone in body, but she's always around when we need her. We call upon her and ask her to help us." And that is what I always tell them. They always remember her and remember the things that she gave us; and I am passing everything that she taught me, I am passing on to my children. The things we do in the Longhouse. Doing the feathers, doing the Rattler, combing people's hair, because this has to be done, and Indian marriage.

My children have had Indian marriage with Justice of the Peace in the Longhouse. This was something I had. I had an Indian marriage, and my daughters, Muriel, Adele, Little Ruby and Sheila followed that step. They had a marriage with the Justice of Peace in the Longhouse, with the Mask Dancers to follow and bless them. That was Frank and Muriel Wilson. And my oldest son, when he got married, he brought his wife; he carried her into my mother's house, carried his wife to my mother's house. And he had two girls from that first marriage; and then his second marriage, he has had six children. Twins and four others: boy, a girl, another boy, another girl, and they are all growing up.

My second-oldest son became a mechanic; and his son from the first marriage, he's got a little boy, my great-grandson, and another two boys with the second marriage, and he has his own mechanic shop, a small, little mechanic shop. My oldest son, he is a fisherman. He likes the outdoors. My youngest son is also a fisherman and he is a carver. I've received some beautiful carvings from two of my children. Sheila, who got married in the Longhouse and has children with her first marriage, two beautiful children, and on her second she's got one son, and she's also a carver. She's carved some beautiful little masks at the beginning. And my youngest son, who has become a carver. I always tell my children that their great-grandfather was a carver, my dad's father. And Dad's grandfather was also a carver—beautiful, his whole house was carved, and I have been looking for that picture. It was all carved inside the little Longhouse, and I always tell them that they should have a skill of that because my dad carved and my grandfather and my great-grandfather, and it showed up in my two younger ones, Sheila and Alphonse. They are carving, and the youngest one of all became an RCMP. She and her husband joined the RCMP and they both became RCMPs. Before she went into the RCMP, she joined the Longhouse, and I wondered about that for a while, and I thought the Indian in her was so strong that she asked to go into the Longhouse. The teachings that she heard from Grandma and Grandpa even though she was very, very young. Then when she joined the RCMP, that gave her more courage to carry on what she went into, the training, the intense training that she went into was carried on. We went to the graduation, and it was beautiful. I went to three graduations—two of hers and one of her husband's. When they entered to become an RCMP, they didn't want to be a special constable. They graduated from college in Merritt, BC. When they entered, they had stressed to them that they weren't there to be special constables for Native People; they wanted to be full-fledged RCMPs, and I was very, very proud of them.[1]

With things that happened—accidents and things that—when I was in the accident and I was in a wheelchair for a long time, with my children helping me, carrying me down, bringing me to the hospital for eighteen months, I made a comeback; I think I have fulfilled all my obligations to my parents' expectations to do what they wanted, do what they asked of me to carry out. I feel that I have done a lot in the short life, and always said that your lifetime is your learning span, and it is true. It's always a learning, your life is your learning span, by giving what you know and handing things down to the young people as a gift, the teachings.

---

1   As of 2020: Oldest son Ron Jr. worked at Crofton Mill; Leo became a mechanic; Muriel (Molly) became a child safety social worker and now a manager; Adele works with youth as a life skills coach; Sheila works in the Cowichan Tribes Finance Department; Little Ruby was an RCMP officer but is now a Hul'q'umi'num' language instructor; Melissa works in the Cowichan Treaty Department.

   Grandchildren: Rachel Henry works at Cowichan Tribes; Carleen August and Lynsey Hwuneem both work in social development at Cowichan Tribes; and Joe Jr. works at Lelumuylh, the Cowichan Tribes Daycare.

I have never denied any of my people who come to me to ask me to give them the teachings of what I know or how to do something, what to do in helping themselves. I have always tried my best and I don't think I will ever stop doing that. I think I will keep on carrying on the wishes of the people, and helping them to get the language is my most important, including my own children, because I feel I let them down by not speaking Indian to them. When I was being punished for speaking the language, I thought I was doing them a favour when I spoke only English to them, later on finding out that it was wrong and trying to correct it; and now it is very, very hard. I am not the only one. There are so many people that did the same; they didn't have to be in residential school, they were in day school, and they had to be punished for being an Indian and were called savages. We were not savages; we were people who were proud people. But they just didn't understand us, and I think to this day it is still the same. There are so many people who don't understand our ways.

I have worked in so many places, from the Band Office to being a councillor for the Band, and then working as a researcher for the Band for the twelve years, and then I worked for the Native Heritage Centre. I met many, many people that were travelling. I was working in a special place where I did basket weaving with cedar and bull rushes and talking about what can be done with the cedar roots and cedar boughs. What you make of cedar boughs—as in making clam baskets. I remember my granddad going into the forest and coming out in half an hour and having a basket made for clams because he was going to go clam digging. The cedar boughs is just split in half, and the same with cedar roots. And cedar—cedar baskets, showing how to peel, separate the cedar from the cedar bark, the inner bark and the out bark. This is all that I did. I enjoyed working there. I sold small baskets. I had one of my small grandchildren there with me working with me and selling little book markers, were a couple of dollars each for themselves.

I worked with the Native Friendship Centre people as an Elder, giving the teachings. Then Malaspina College as night school as teacher for the language. I have worked with Professor Hukari for many years, since 1973, and various other people that he sent to me.

And we worked together teaching some people to become language teachers who had a couple of—we had a whole year, a nine-month course, and the same with the one that was at the Band Office. I have enjoyed working with my sister at South Island, whom I worked with for the past three years. I worked with Cowichan Tribes Child and Family Services, and Native Justice,[2] which was very interesting. Child and Family Services, La'lumutul' Smun'eem, who I am still working with. I enjoy working with them. Giving them advice about the best way to handle certain areas of looking after our people.

I have been involved with many of the people around our area who come to me for help. People from Vancouver, who have or whom I have known for many years, always contact me and call me to their homes to help them. Go there for blessing of their house, hwqw'uqwiils after a death, or burn food for the deceased, burning clothes, or when something happens to their dancer, they call me. And these are all special areas that I feel important that you have to learn on your own. And it is all from the teachings that we received from my mother and my dad, who were very special people.

I have really enjoyed working with people. I always welcome people to my home, whether it's spiritually or just advice. I welcome and I help them do whatever they may need. I am sure my children will carry out all the things that I have asked them to, which they have already started doing. They have already carried out the things that I can't do anymore. Because of my health, I cannot go to the Longhouse, so they have taken over that area for me, and I have to be just in the background and giving them advice about what goes on. I work with my brother closely and my sister to do anything that goes. If there is anything that goes wrong, I go to them and talk to them. I also thank them for being close to me.

I always have prayers in my heart for our Native People.

February 1998

---

2 The South Island Justice Project was started in the 1990s. Ruby was one of the members of the Council of the Sul'wheen (Elders). The project is no longer in existence.

Index

Page numbers in bold indicate a photograph or information in a photograph's caption. Plate numbers are indicated by **pl**.

James, Cyrus (Ruby Peter's uncle), 90, 91, 92

Joe, Adele Sti'tum'atye' (Ruby Peter's daughter), **129**, 160n, **pl12, pl15, pl17**

Joe, Muriel (née Alphonse). *See* Hwuneem, Muriel (Molly) (née Alphonse) (Ruby Peter's sister)

Johnny, Sheila Qwulsimtunaat (Ruby Peter's daughter), **129**, 159, 160, **pl15, pl25**

Kamloops Residential School, 23
knitting, 26, 65, 68, 92, 149
Kuper Island Residential School, **24**, 25
kw'unt'als (basalt), 79–80, 79n, 111

Leo, Cecilia Qwulsimtunaat:
alcohol use and recovery, 16–17, 31; with Basil Alphonse, **6, 15, pl23**; on being a woman, 66; on being Thi'tha, 40–41, 59–60, 86, 98–99; on burning of food, 39; cautions about sexual abuse, 70, 71–75; on cultural differences, 80; education, 25, 58, 85; end of life, 158; with family, **15**; family background, 7–8, 77–78, 87–88; family song, 43–44; first marriage, 8–11, 86–87; as foster mother, 33–34; on hard times, 64; Kamloops trip, 144–46; knitting, 26, 65, 66, 67, 92; on learning traditions, 32–33; on marriage, 59, 77, 78, 86–87; and Norman Spahan, 149, 150; on perfection in all things, 69; on prayers, 54; pregnancy and children, 13–14; on raising children, 114, 118; and Ruby Peter's house, 124, 125; and Ruby Peter's Longhouse experience, 137; and Ruby Peter's pregnancies, 103–4; second marriage, 13; son's death,

16, 29–31; teaching weaving, **69**; teachings about play, 26–27, 60; treats broken collarbone, 20

Little Joe (Ruby Peter's uncle), 120, 124, 125, 126

logging camp, stay at, 130–31

Longhouse: Cecilia Leo's different teachings, 109; and cultural identity, 84, 155; initiation, 34–36; Ruby Peter's experience in, 138–40; winter dances, 154. *See also* identity; teachings, cultural and traditional

Louie, Delores Swustanulwut (Ruby Peter's sister), 14, 23, **27**, 30, 147, 148, **pl4, pl15, pl18**

marriages: Cecilia Leo's teachings on, 32–33, 77; family involvement, 7, 8, 60, 89, 100; life with in-laws, 86–87; suitable partners, 59–60, 78, 87, 98, 99; traditional and church/legal, 82, 159, **pl25**; traditional proposal, 81–82; women, and reserve membership, 8

Masked Dance, 42–43, 59–60, 62–63

Masked Dancers: and marriage, 159; origin story, 17; and Rattler, 42; responsibilities, 156; Sxwuyxwi, 17, 33, 43, 62, 63, 84, 155

masks: banned, 62–63, 62n, 84, 152, 153, 156; passing down of, 42–43, 44; purpose, 17; and songs, 43

Melissa (Ruby Peter's daughter). *See* Shelby, Melissa Wuswasulwut (Ruby Peter's daughter)

memorials, 36–37, 39, 40, 42. *See also* funerals

Michel, Cecilia (Ruby Peter's grandmother), **9**

mourning, and release, 37

murder, at Kuper Island, 117

names, Indian, 7, 42, 43, 91–92, 154, 156

Native Indian Teachers Education Program (NITEP), 147, 147n

ochre (tumulh), 17, 38, 39, 47, 48–49, 113
Old People: on alcohol, 22–23; care of, 116–17, 120–23, 125, 128–30; and end of Ruby Peter's marriage, 146; on helping others, 2–3; on identity, 17; on raising children, 114; in story of Shne'um, 51–52; on witchcraft, 56. *See also* Elders
oral tradition, and written account, xii, xiii, xiv–xv

parents, loss of, 17–18, 38, 56, 112–13
Paul, William Wushq, 34, 61, 117
Peter, Alphonse Taxwulthut (Ruby Peter's son), **129**, 160
Peter, Leo Benjamin Hwuneem (Ruby Peter's son), 127–28, **129,** 160n, **pl9, pl15**
Peter, Molly Stu'matulwut, v, ix–x, **129,** 160n, **pl9, pl12, pl15, pl16**
Peter, Ron Jr. (Ruby Peter's son), **129,** 160n, **pl27**
Peter, Ronald (Ruby Peter's husband): alcohol use, 106–7, 131, 137, 142; apologizes, 140–41; barn building, 117; at daughter's wedding, **pl25**; house, 136, 137; logging, 100, 105; marriage ends, 143, 146; marries Ruby Peter, 100, **102**
Peter, Ruby Sti'tum'atul'wut, **xxii**; as activist, xi, xii; on alcohol use, 2, 22–23, 31, 46, 48, 97, 131, 141; on barn building, 116–17, 118; baskets, **xvi,** 161, **pl1**; breaks collarbone, 20; brother's death, 16, 29–31; care of Old People, 116–17, 120–23, 125, 128–30; as child, **14, 15**; children and their families, ix, **129,** 158–60,

160n, 162, 168–69, **pl16, pl17, pl20, pl25, pl26, pl27, pl28, pl29, pl30**; on coming of age rituals, 78–80; as councillor, 107, 120, 123, 136; Cowichan Honouring, **pl12, pl13, pl14, pl15**; on cultural identity: 83–84, 153–57, 159; on cultural identity, passing on, 44–45, 48, 78, 107–8, 162; on cultural teachings, 1–2, 109–114; on decisions and acceptance, 99, 124, 125; with Delores, **pl4, pl18**; experience in Longhouse, 138–40; family background, 7–8, 17, 59–60, 71, 89, 90–92; on family songs, 43–44; farm work, 85, 104, 105; as foster parent, 118, 131–35, 142; goes to carnival, 88–89; grandparents, 8, **9,** 11, 12, 13, 37, 75–76, 81–82; health concerns, 131, 135, 137–38, 142, 143, 160, 162; on helping people, 13, 54–57, 160, 162; honorary degrees, ix, xiii, **pl4, pl9, pl10, pl11, pl19, pl20, pl21**; houses of, 100–101, 105, 117, 118, 123–26, 136; Kamloops trip, 144–46; knitting and spinning, 65, 68, 149; lifetime as learning span, 160–61; on marriage, 59–60, 81–82, 86–87; marriage ends, 143, 145, 146, 147; married life of, 100–101, **102,** 106–7, 126, 140–41; mother's teachings about play, 26–27, 60; mother's teachings on tradition, 32–33, 59; on murder on Kuper Island, 117–18; and Norman Spahan, 149–51, **pl7**; on not talking about what you belong to, 45–46; physical abuse of, 137–38, 141–42, 143, 146; pregnancies of, 103–5; preparing tule, **pl24**; on raising children, 2, 3, 114, 118–19; on Rattler, 42–44; on repetition in teaching, 86;